ATTEMPTING ADULT

Faith

Faith Hancock has spent quite a long time drifting through life, waiting for the right moment for fame and glory to strike so she can swan off to buy a mansion. She has worked for years at writing words for other people, and has now decided to write her own and see how that pans out.

She has also succumbed to biology and is now a proud parent of the most awesome child in the world (yes, it really *is* better than all the other ones. Fight me.)

Faith now lives in the middle of nowhere with an ancient smelly dog, a cat that falls off tables, some small feathery descendants of the dinosaurs, and the aforementioned Awesome Child. She's very happy, thank you very much, but she really wouldn't mind that mansion someday soon.

Her book *Caravan Cooking* is also published by Tiger of the Stripe.

William

William's words give power to the helpless, embolden the meek, provide sustenance to those that hunger, and comfort to those that fear. He's a man, he's a legend – and he can't avoid talking absolute nonsense in his biography. He still can't believe that someone would be crazy enough to publish a single word that he has written.

Mother Nature neglected to provide William with a mind's eye (he has Aphantasia – Google it) so he can't see what he's trying to describe to anyone else, and he has no memory, so even if he does manage to remember what he's talking about he's forgotten it by the next chapter.

William lives in Somerset, currently. He has also previously lived not in Somerset and, due to procreation, has a houseful of pet rats. That'll teach him.

Roxanne

Roxanne has always had a love for illustration and takes inspiration from books that she used to read as a child.

After studying GCSE Art and Design, she continued her learning, studying A-Level Art alongside Art History and Photography. It took a while to figure out which road she wanted to take but after the birth of her daughter, her love of book illustrations was re-discovered.

Roxanne is the only one of us, apart from Publisher Guy, who has actually followed a sensible path to get to where she wants. She agreed to illustrate this book because she fancied a giggle, and because she has a bet to see which one of the authors succumbs to the horrors of fame and fortune and ends up in rehab first.

ATTEMPTING ADULTHOOD

Faith Hancock

and

William Collins

with illustrations by

Roxanne Knott

TIGER OF THE STRIPE

TIGER OF THE STRIPE · RICHMOND

MMXXIII

First published in 2023 by
TIGER OF THE STRIPE
50 Albert Road
Richmond
Surrey TW10 6DP
United Kingdom

tigerofthestripe.co.uk

ISBN 978-1-904799-75-7

Typeset in the United Kingdom by
Tiger of the Stripe

Contents

Faith ii

William ii

Roxanne ii

Acknowledgements   I

Introduction   3

Life In General   5

School   8

Little School 9

Big School 9

College II

Career   I3

Money   I7

Bills   20

Love Life   23

Sex 25

Dating 27

Co-Habitation 3I

Marriage 32

Splitting Up 34

Parenthood   37

To Breed Or Not To Breed? 38

Babies 40

Toddlers 44

Tweens 47

Teenagers 47

Wider Family   51

Parents 52

Grandparents 54

Siblings 55

Cousins 56

Aunts and Uncles 56

Housing   58

Rent 61

Buy 62

Maintenance 64

DIY 65

Décor 66

Garden 67

Veggies 67

Flowers 69

Wild 70

Landscaping 71

Pets   72

Dog 74

Cat 75

Rabbit 75

Hamster 75

Gerbil 76

Guinea Pig 76

Rat 77

Snake 77

Spider 77

Fish 78

Birds 78

Cars   79

Driving 80

Maintenance 81

Fixing 81

Health   83

Appearance   87

Ageing 88

Hair 90

Skin 94

Body Shape 95

Food   99

Hobbies   105

Reading 106

Writing 106

Drawing 106

Music 107

Painting 107

Walking 108

Dancing 108

Making Things 108

Foraging 109

Cooking 109

Gaming 109

Sport   111

Football 113

Rugby 113

Cricket 114

Tennis 114

Swimming 114

Cycling 115

Boxing 115

Gymnastics 115

Ice Skating 116

Equestrian 116

Politics   117

    Conservatives 120

    Labour 120

    Lib Dems 121

    Green Party 121

    SNP 122

    Socialists 122

Religion   124

Technology   128

    Televison 130

    Computers 131

    The Internet 133

    Social Media 134

Festivities   137

    Birthdays 138

    Easter 139

    May Day 140

    Hallowe'en 141

    Christmas 142

    New Year's Day 143

    Weddings 144

    Funerals 145

The Wider World   147

Conclusion   151

Acknowledgements

Thanks to everyone who contributed stories and anecdotes to this book, knowingly or otherwise. Please don't sue me if you recognise your life and I didn't ask you for permission first.

Biggest thanks and love to my wonderful girl, who not only made the Parenting chapter credible, but who also managed to learn how to (almost) sleep through the night so that writing this book was possible.

Huge gratitude to Jon Hancock, who combed this book with his scholarly Red Pen for typos and sentences ending in prepositions, Up With Which He Will Not Put.

And finally, thank you to my wonderful long-suffering Mr Publisher. The amount extra of work I have given him is enough to slay a small donkey, yet still he continues to punish himself by publishing my books.

Introduction

So, to conclude,[1] we don't really have much more of a clue about how to run ourselves than you do. We're just better at typing.[2]

This may seem a rather unusual/brave/stupid way to start a book that is supposed to be giving you tips on how to get through life as unscathed and unbroken as possible,[3] but as we progressed with this work it panned out that it was more a book of warnings than a book of help.

We tried – oh how we tried! But the more we wrote the more obvious it became that every single life is different. Every single one of the 7.9 billion of them.[4] And we could only really give hints on how to get through *our* lives. And we're already doing that.

So, this is more a book of suggestions, advice, anecdotes that make us look even more stupid than you, pitfalls to avoid, and minor victories to grab with both hands when you get the chance.

In the interests of diversity, we have written this from the point of view of a slightly less useless woman, and a slightly less useful man. If you buy this book and make us rich, we'll include more genders for the sequel. We also include some comments from our irascible, right-wing publisher, to balance our fervent, left-wing rantings. You'll know it's him, because he speaks like this.

This book is really just to empower you, dear reader, to realise that You Can Do This, and you don't really need our help, or anyone else's. Actually, that doesn't really bode well for the sequel, does it? How about you tell your mates to buy that one, even though YOU won't need it. You'll be so perfect, and balanced and happy

---

1   Or rather, to begin, Miss Hancock.
2   Not guaranteed.
3   Spoiler alert, no one does.
4   This was wrong even as I typed it. Not much I can do about that.

by then, from reading this one, that any suggestion you give will be pounced on like a deer carcass in a lion cage.[5] So, basically, everyone's a winner.

---

[5] Isn't that what you've always wanted to be?

Life In General

Ahh, life… That glorious institution in which we are lucky enough to partici-pate! (Well, I'm assuming you are still participating, otherwise you wouldn't be reading this. If, somehow, you are reading this from beyond the grave, could you possibly see your way towards sending me the winning lottery numbers? Pleaseandthankyou.)

There are no instructions. Not for those who made us, or indeed for ourselves. I am beginning to think the Buddhists are right, and this isn't our first time around. We're secondhand from some cosmic eBay; otherwise we'd arrive in a lovely box (ok, some of us sort of do) with some folded instructions and an Allen key, as opposed to a complete lack of ideas and a great big messy splat.

Anyway. Life is great, isn't it?

But (there's always one of those)…

Sometimes it can be confusing, terrifying, completely overwhelming, joyful, heartbraking, intense, wonderful, and you may be standing helplessly in the ruins of your mind, wondering what the hell happened to staying up with your friends, eating pizza and playing video games.

How are you supposed to juggle work, a house, a family, friends, and a rapidly deteriorating mental state, without an injection of a million quid and a personal therapist?[6]

I'll let you into a secret...

No one knows. Literally all of us are totally winging it, and hoping no one else ever finds out. I can pretty much guarantee that behind every sane, sensible seeming human being who has apparently got their shit together is NOT 'a good man/woman/dog/trust fund,' but a whole lifetime of baggage and craziness that they have not yet dealt with, and probably won't ever get around to doing so – because the rest of Life gets in the way! Argh! How do we even manage to get out of bed and continue functioning?

We do this because we generally try to forget our issues; or they are so hidden by that gigantic pile of washing up, or the work deadline, or the screaming kids, that it gets shelved along with other important things such as:

How is Keith Richards still alive?

If Casey is riding along in a train going at 45 mph, how many oranges will she have left at the end of the journey if she gives three to Shannon and they are both wearing green?

Did my hamster actually go to live on a lovely farm when I was 5, or is the fabric of life unravelling before my very eyes?

So, you can either go on through life as you are – and I'm sure you're doing a great job – or you can choose to have a mid (or early, or late-, we're not judging) life crisis. In fact, studies show that the vast majority of us will have at least one of these throughout our lives, and there really is no shame in it. Therapy should be widely available to absolutely everyone, because it turns out we're all a little bit bonkers and really need some qualified help to see us through the beautiful journey we call Life.

If you don't have a therapist, you can still get through it – you may just rely a little more on long suffering friends and family to help get you by, and help you get back on track. If none of these people can help you, you can still definitely win at life. Just remember one of the most important things in this entire world:

---

6   Preferably someone professional, sympathetic and very good at their jobs, while being so utterly beautiful that you can fantasise about them without ever having to worry about whether they'd stoop to doing anything physical with you, thus compounding your issues.

Do whatever you like, as long as you're not a dick.[7]

It's pretty much that simple. It's YOUR life, you can literally do whatever you want it with it, as long as you aren't hurting, maiming or killing anyone else.[8,9] Don't listen to anyone who tells you what or what not to do with your life – you follow your own heart and your own dreams. This will make you far happier than doing what someone else thinks you ought to be doing.

Try to help people as much as you can, but don't be a doormat. Stand up for yourself, without being a knob. Look after yourself and make sure you are healthy and well – but don't do this to the exclusion of everything else in this life that might be fun or a little bit naughty. Chocolate is fine, as is wine. Sex is also fun. Be a good person and try to make sure there is a planet left for all the people who will be alive after you're dead.[10,11]

---

[7]　Having one is fine, in both senses.

[8]　Or kittens. We're a big fan of kittens, so be as nice to them as you possibly can, please.

[9]　*Less of this mawkish sentimentality, please, young lady! But no doubt you were thinking of the Ancren Riwl in which we learn that the Anchorite sisters were allowed to keep no animal except a cat: 'ȝe mine lēove sustren, ne schulen haben nō bēst, būte kat ōne.'*

[10]　*You have managed to leave this page uncommonly empty, Miss Hancock.* You're the one in charge of typesetting, Mr Publisher. I'm merely a humble writer. *Humble, my foot!*

[11]　I would have filled it, but the mention of chocolate, sex and wine reminded me of something urgent I had to do.

School

'The best years of your life!' they say.[12] 'You have so much to look forward to! So much to give! You should enjoy these years with unparalleled enthusiasm and great joy!'

If you're like most school kids, you greet these words with a polite smile and an inner eye roll. What do they know?

For some, school is marvellous. For those with confidence, looks, a nice home life and a bit of money behind them – basically the tools required for a successful life – school can provide the perfect foundations for a successful life.

For other people, who lack such abilities and instead excel in more unorthodox areas, such as being a bit short or going bright red if anyone dares talk to them, this can just be a training school for how to get beaten up.

Of course, these are the extremes, and most of us fit somewhere in the middle. Not over-performing, not under-performing. Just existing. The perfect zone for getting mostly ignored.

---

[12]   They lie.

Of course, what 'they' don't tell you about school is that it is a battleground; the excuse of 'getting an education' is just so that your parents could get a break. They waved you off merrily, aware of but ignoring the fact that you would fight some of your hardest battles in the school yard, before collapsing on the sofa with a glass of gin after the school run, cackling gleefully.

Little School

This is generally a fun place to be, filled with lots of poster paints and pictures of ladybirds on the walls. Teachers are kind, learning is fun, and you get to go home halfway through the day. If you were one of the lucky ones, you started school with a collection of cohorts in nursery, then went up to Big School with them, so at least you knew people. But, even this came with its drawbacks. What if you wanted to break out of your friendship group? What if one of the Popular Kids started to make advances, but you couldn't possibly sit on the bench with them as you'd made an I HATE THEM club with Greg and Emma three years ago? You'd have to shave your head, dye your eyebrows and pretend you didn't speak English in order to make your getaway.

Big School

You all start out in the same scared, confused state, then generally latch onto another child – somebody, ANYBODY who could make you feel like less of a lonely loner. This usually turned out to be the other freak in the class, though they often had more bodily hygiene issues than you, so you were forced to endure noses being held and cries of 'FARRRRRT!' every time you and your 'friend' made an entrance.[13]

Secondary school is basically some kind of David Attenborough documentary – the Popular stalking the Weirdos like lions hunting gazelle. If you fit into neither of these groups, your best bet is to freeze and hope that their vision is based on movement, leaving you ignored in favour of some more energetic prey.

If you were one of the Popular Kids, I... don't really know what to say to you. It's nice that you were gifted some great genes and the sort of personality that made you charming and attractive to other teenagers,[14] but could you not have been slightly nicer to the rest of the scum that you trod down with your designer

---

13 I am very glad to say that nothing of that nature ever happened at my school.
14 Personality disorders, anyone?

trainers? Maybe some people don't actually enjoy being taunted every single day in order to make you feel better about yourself.

We know, now, that you only did this because you were consumed with an echoing void where your hearts should be, or maybe you literally had no idea how to be nice to people – but we could have helped with that.

Life is not about destroying people so that you can make a tower to the top with their bones and entrails. Just sayin'. Hopefully your kids will be nicer than you were.

Keep your head down, coast along, and look forward to a time when you can actually be yourself without someone taking umbrage to it.

Being good at the subjects won't help you either, oh no, far from it! If you have a modicum of brains, you will have to hide them better than Debbie from 9F hid the fact that she shagged Liam from 10D behind the maths department.

Being Good At School is something that should definitely be hidden, and practised in secret, in the same way that you smile sweetly at your parents and tell them you are studying with a friend, when in reality you are going to walk into town in your skimpiest outfits and see how many lorry drivers beep at you.

But, Not Being Good At School won't help you either, as the Careers Advisor will repeatedly tell you. It's a fine line between succeeding at the rest of your life, and getting through school without getting your head kicked in or developing mental health issues that will ruin the next 60 odd years of your existence.[15]

And then, having been taught Latin, Pythagoras and the entirely guessed meaning to some poems written millennia before you were born, without even a hint as to how a bank account/washing machine/email scam works, you're out on your ear with a collection of letters on bits of paper and absolutely no clue what to do next.

Seriously, why is school so shit? If they actually wanted to educate us, they would teach us how to deal with Council Tax reminders and when to put your bins out. We might be taught that this is all a gigantic waste of time, and we'd be better off doing some sort of menial job to make money, while saving the rest of our life and talents to do something we actually enjoy. Or, raising us to realise that the best thing we can do is just be nice, and grow veggies.

Because, let's face it, when the Zombie Apocalypse finally hits, who's going to care how many Shakespeare sonnets you can analyse, or how many points of Pi you can identify? The square route of what now? This will be no use to you when

---

[15]   I can well believe that the next 60 years of your existence will be odd, Miss Hancock. It is a natural consequence of vegetarianism.

you are jabbing at an undead being's brain with the nearest sharp pointy thing that comes to hand.

College

Now we're talking. You are considered responsible enough to make your own way there, and some of you may even have started driving (see Cars). You can call your teachers by their first names, and wear whatever the hell you want. You suddenly start feeling like you can break out of the mould you have spent the last 10 years occupying. You now have Serious Decisions to make about what exams you will sit, which will lead you on seamlessly into your future career.

This thought frequently keeps me awake at night:[16] Who on earth decided that you have to decide what you want to do with your whole entire life by the time you are 16? Most of us don't even know what day it is, or how to cross the road effectively, by this point. What's with all the pressure? Things, life, and especially people, change so vastly between the ages of 16 and 20 – hell, even between the ages of 16 and 17 – that it is totally unfair to stuff them into a little 'career' box and send them on their merry way. After all, most kids want to be astronauts, vets, or simply 'grown up' when you ask them when they're small. That changes a lot between the ages of being totally incontinent and being able to interact with other humans,[17] so who is to say that career aspirations don't change a lot in that time too?

I'm pretty old now, and I'm still upset – on behalf on my unformed self, and on behalf of the countless other unformed selves – at the idea of being forced to consider a potential career that would take up my whole life, when I was still pretty much a child. I received some advice when I was 16, that pretty much changed my entire life. I will share it with you now. Are you ready? It's pretty momentous... Do. What. Makes. You. Happy.

And that's it! Pretty simple, huh? But it's actually pretty earth shaking at the same time.

When I received this advice I was desperate, DESPERATE to be a vet. It had been my one and only dream since I could understand that sometimes pussycats and doggies need a doctor too. I was going to be that doctor! I would spend my grown up years mending broken creatures, and end up taking most of them

---

16   This is a lie. – Be careful, Miss Hancock, I do not tolerate mendacity.
17   And then, eventually, becoming totally incontinent again.

home to live in my massive mansion/farmhouse.[18] However, in order to be a good vet you have to be good at a few specific school subjects. One of those I was not good at. So not good, in fact, that it regularly reduced me to tears of rage and impotence, and I had to have a tutor to help me scrape through GCSE maths.

Still, I ignored this pretty important stumbling block, and got myself a Saturday job in a local vet. I loved it; holding pussycats' paws and learning how to inject things, and being helped to figure out which end of a dog is which. I had a heart to heart with the vet nurse one morning, wailing about how I'd picked Physics, Biology, Chemistry and Maths for my A Levels – all of which I hated, except Biology. Debbie, in her customary breezy fashion, said,

'Ah pickle. It'll be fine. Just do what makes you happy.'

All of a sudden, I was free.

Those six little words released me from my self-imposed misery, and I instantly changed my A levels to English, French and Art – with a Biology AS level thrown in, just in case. I'm still not a vet, and pretty happy about it.

Striving for the future is massively important, of course. But, as any Buddhist will tell you, being happy right now is even more important. What if you get hit by a bus on the way to becoming happy, when you could have been happy doing the thing that made you happy, rather than going for the thing that you THINK might make you happy? I realise this is a very involved sentence, which may be seen as a bit of a defeatist one, but actually it makes loads of sense!

Daydreaming and planning and thinking ahead are important things, of course. But, being happy is importanter, in my opinion.[19]

---

[18] See Career, and Housing.

[19] I fear, Miss Hancock, that the opinion of anyone who thinks that the comparative of 'important' is 'importanter' carries very little weight, even in these benighted times. How would I ever be able to hold my head up high at a gathering of the Wynkyn de Worde Society, the Galley Club, the Stationers' Company, the Bibliographical Society or the Double Crown Club (should any of these august bodies ever deign to invite me to become a member), if I let such a solecism slip through unreprimanded? It is clear that the barbarians are no longer at the gates; they are seated before the fire in my favourite armchair, eating my crumpets and, very probably, wearing my slippers. Do you think your slippers would fit me? No!

Career

Despite the previous chapter and because of the following ones, you are going to have to get yourself one of these. Sorry.

Just imagine loving your life and your earning capabilities so much that you would leap out of bed every morning, filled with all the beans and all the joys of Spring, ready to take on the world with the love and exuberance that fill your heart! That's the dream, isn't it – to get paid enough to survive whilst doing something that you ACTUALLY like.

However,[20] life isn't often like this. Most of us have to unwillingly haul ourselves out of our warm beds, at a disgusting time of day, to go and spend the majority of the daylight hours doing something that at best bores us, and at worst makes us

---

[20]   Yes, this really is just a fancy word for another one of those Buts. – *But me no buts, please, Miss Hancock.*

feel we'd rather be doing a jazz workshop or learning how to stick pins into our most painful orifices.

Jobs. Ugh. Unfortunately, these are likely to happen to you at some point in life, like measles or dating someone that turns out to be a proper toolbag.[21] We were never told that we'd have to actually go out and do something unspeakable, just so that we could afford to eat and pay for that roof over our heads! Were we? Pretty sure I was never included in that memo. I thought you patiently got through the drudgery and misery of school, then you were released to shower the world with your awesomeness and get showered with money in return.

No. Sadly, it doesn't work like this.

Unfortunately, unlike the measles/toolbag situation, society today pretty much demands that you have one of these to avoid starving in a cave somewhere. In theory toolbag dating, assuming said toolbag is rich, can negate your need for employment. But firstly, it still means you have to live with a toolbag, and secondly this is unlikely to happen early enough in your life to prevent your need to, at some stage, be employed.

If you are one of those lucky, lucky people that already know they want to be a professional tight rope walker/wedding planner/topiaryist[22] by the age of six months and is then able to spend the rest of their youth achieving this dream then 'jobs' is likely to in fact be singular, and awesome. But research has shown that of the 7.9 billion people currently wandering around ruining our planet, only twelve know what they hell they actually want to do in life,[23] and at least eight of those are too busy having pointless arguments on Facebook to actually get on with it.

You might be one of those people who has A Plan, and has worked their way steadily towards achieving said Plan, following all the right school processes and hitting all the targets to get the job that you've always wanted. Those people happen to jobs; for the rest of us, jobs generally happen to us.

You might also have no clue what you want to do, and will just take any job that is vaguely related to your non existent Plan, eventually ending up close to it in a way that doesn't make you too miserable. You bounce around from stacking boxes in a food factory to serving customers in a small boutique shop selling painted teaspoons, and rarely go home with any sense of fulfilment.

---

[21] This does not refer to a person that uses a bag of tools in their employment. They are generally a darn good bet.

[22] If this wasn't a word, it is now. – It certainly is not, young lady. You'll never win at Scrabble with an attitude like that! The correct term is 'topiarist'.

[23] This does not include getting drunk. The number of people who know they want to get drunk is astronomical.

You may also have no Plan at all, but realise that you still need to make money in order to survive in this day and age. Have you thought about dating a rich toolbag?[24] Any one of these things is absolutely fine.

When you're young, you go to work simply to pay for pleasures when you aren't at work. Those cheap bottles of spirits, experimental drugs and packets of condoms that you're probably never going to get to use don't buy themselves. So you turn up to work in a place that pays you almost zero whilst making an absolute fortune for the owner before heading down to the bus stop/park/pub/club, and spending the whole lot in approximately two hours. Rinse repeat... And suddenly you're 20-ish.

By now you may have snagged yourself a partner. This brings in the first level of proper adulting. A slight hint of responsibility. A future to save for. Maybe a house. A pension for when you're... No, wait, he/she's dumped you, back to the paying for pleasures until you're twenty-five. Responsibility can go on the back burner[25] for now.

You get a bit older, maybe find yourself another partner. Maybe you've moved in together and started doing proper adult stuff like shopping, planning meals or occasionally staying sober in the evening. But, your life needs to move forward. This requires a job upgrade. McDonalds is going to have to survive without you.[26] This is probably going to mean an office.You start slaving away in the office environment for a few years. Maybe in the same one, maybe in a few, and you've noticed one availing truth;[27] it's the loud ones that get on. It's not the ones that actually, quietly do their work really bloody well, it's the loud, overconfident ones, that actually do naff all of any use to the company that get the promotions and all that extra cash. Every single bloody time. So you carry on slogging away, making a bit more than before but still with the same chilling sense that you're wasting your life.

A bit later on comes the crunch time. Kids, mortgage, pension, bill, Bills, BILLS have happened and you've worked your way up enough to be comfortable. Too comfortable to do anything about the fact that you'd rather stay at home and pull your pubic hair out one by one with tweezers than go to work. Do you jack it

---

24   There we go again, Miss Hancock. I have no idea what this term means, but I suspect it must be something unsavoury.

25   The unlit back burner because you can't afford logs.

26   Probably until about 7 days after you retire.

27   No, no! This will not do, Miss Hancock. The word you want is not 'availing,' though what you do want, I cannot say. Perhaps you mean 'abiding'.

all in, take the kids out of school and live in a van in Scotland instead? Do you? You're tempted, but you won't. Trust me.

Then comes the most depressing part about this whole thing. You're in a job you don't detest too much; it pays you enough to be able to survive, but still your soul yearns for the days when you had hopes and dreams. But all you get to do now is work, work, work, retire, die.[28]

Unless you are incredibly rich, or happy to live in a tent in the woods, you are going to need a job to pay for things. Until society collapses or the Zombie Apocalypse finally gets here and we have to concentrate on hitting the next zombie rather than hitting the next pointless deadline, making money is a good survival technique.

There are, also, a lot of completely pointless jobs that are created, apparently, to give some people a chance to feel as though they are worth something. What on earth *is* HR, anyway? And have you ever heard of a Dessert Artist? I mean, really. It's like these things are simply invented to give the guys who interpret the Census a bit of a giggle.

The other side of this is that a lot of jobs are now being destroyed by machinery (see Technology). In the old days you would go the the shop, buy your bits and bobs, trundle to the cashier place – and have an actual interaction with another human being. Nowadays, Tesco are getting lazy and expecting you to do all their work for them. Countless people have lost useful stepping stone jobs, and thousands of people are missing that bit of chat and excuse for a social that they got when having a chat with a shop person.

---

[28]   Probably about 7 days after you retire.

Money

This stuff is a gosh darn horrible thing, isn't it? If you have it, you're always striving for more of it, and if you don't have it then you're always striving for, well, ANY of it. We thought we'd precede the next chapters with this one because, as it turns out, you're probably going to need a fair bit of it in order to get through Life.

Money started out as a bartering system: You want a house built, you enlist your neighbours, and you pay them in chickens, or potatoes, or camels, or wives.[29]

---

[29] Though this may or may not be an acceptable barter – better check with all parties involved before you start swapping your spouse for a car.

Then, once people started running out of chickens, potatoes, camels and wives, the bartering system was replaced with chunks of 'precious' metals. This puzzled the peasants, because you couldn't eat the stuff, you couldn't build a house with it[30] and it was useless handing it to other people who had nothing to eat in exchange for it.

Did you know, there used to be a culture in the world whose wealth was literally huge rocks? No one could lift them, so they didn't actually exchange them at all, just assumed that the one with the biggest rock was the richest one who deserved all the Stuff. There is still some of this incredible 'wealth' buried deep under a sea somewhere, and if you could trace your DNA back to them, you might suddenly find yourself living a life of luxury. Give it a try, and remember your faithful author in your will.

Money these days follows pretty much this same principle. It all gets sent to the bank, unless you are a 'hide it under the mattress'[31] type. Once there, the bank uses your hard earned cash to invest in dodgy deals, buy and sell weapons to other countries who would be so much better without our input, or pour money into various nefarious deals. The numbers you see on the screen that correlate to your riches are literally just that – numbers on a screen. If everyone decided to take out all our money all at once, there would not be enough to go around – even Jeff Bezos would struggle to actually count out his wealth in physical form.[32]

Basically, we all turned into Gollum, jealously guarding our relatively useless[33] hoards and turning pale and weird with the effort of hiding it from everyone else, muttering between our fingers as we feverishly count it, and biting the heads off passing fish or children.

The problem, in a nutshell, is Capitalism. This hideous principle was formulated by Adam Smith, but the idea has been around since the 16th century. What a great plan, in theory – pay people to work, sell things that they want, and eventually the whole system is like a great, self-perpetuating circle, with everyone being happy at the end of it. Doesn't quite work that way though, does it?

Nowadays, most of the wealth is hoarded by the most Gollum-like of all of us, with the majority of the people in varying degrees of struggle. It's as though the richest among us fear they will lose all their power if they, for example, shared

---

[30]   Although I think someone probanly has by now, haven't they?

[31]   Actually, it seems like this may not be quite such a terrible idea... although it is if your currency consists of massive rocks.

[32]   Let's face it, he'd struggle to ever find the time in his lifetime to count it. And just imagine if he lost count and had to start all over again.

[33]   Gollum's hoard was considerably less useless though, wasn't it?

a wee bit of it around the poorest of us. Did you know that a billion pounds, sitting in a bank account, makes an interest of around a million pounds a year.[34,35] Obviously this will fluctuate depending on interest rates and where you deposited it,[36] but I think we can all agree that this is a LOT of money.

There should be a rule that if you have a billion pounds, you should donate, at the very least, the interest of it. There are quite a few billionaires now, so that's a good few school dinners. If any politicians are reading this, feel free to take my ideas and run with them... Oh no, wait – you guys are part of the problem. For god's sake, grow a conscience!

---

[34] I assume you are talking about an American billion, 10^9, not the traditional billion, 10^{12}. Even so, your weakness in Mathematics (if you forgive me for saying so, my dear Miss Hancock) lets you down. No self-respecting billionaire (if, indeed, there is such a thing) would accept being paid a mere £1m per annum interest on £1bn (even the American kind); that is an interest rate of 0.1%. While some financial institutions might fob off a poorish person with that sort of rate, they would pay much more handsomely to get their hands on £1bn.

[35] I *told* you I was useless at Mathematics, Mr Publisher. This is why I'm a thorn in your side, not removing thorns from pussy cats' and puppies' paws.

[36] And if it's under the mattress, it won't actually make you anything – except much higher off the floor than before. – I have long suspected, Miss Hancock, that you are the Princess and the Pea. If I planted a single 10 shilling note (well, no, we had better say £5 note) below a hundred mattresses, I believe it would still keep you awake.

Bills

The absolute bane of existence. They drop on the doormat[37] with a plop, like little paper fun-ruiners. Every. Single. Day. The slow drip of your hard-earned cash winging its way to someone considerably richer than you.

But the thing is, life has been very carefully constructed to make bills unavoidable. Unavoidable once you've started them. Internet, TV channels, music subscriptions, audio books, computer game subscriptions, mobile phone contracts,

---

[37] Ok, I know it's inbox these days, but that doesn't sound as good.

magazine subscriptions to build your own nuclear warhead in only 24 issues. Before you had them, you didn't need them, Now you've had them, you can't live without them.[38]

But, due to the power of the internet, you can shop around! Everything's cheaper because of the plethora of competition. And yes, I can see that. You can see that. But you still have to pay for EVERYTHING, all the time, and the internet is so enormous that it really isn't easy.

Previously you'd go to the shop that was appropriate for your required item. Music shop, game shop, sex shop – you'd go there, choose the one you want and buy it. Not now. Everything from electricity to music subscriptions can be garnered from many different places and as for the sex shop... That's pretty much the rest of the internet.

The plethora of options makes it almost 100% likely that you won't get the best value.

Bills will happen, unless you're happy living in the back of cave off moss and spiders, and even then there's probably a subscription service.[39]

Obviously, not all bills are created equal. There are some that we mind paying less than we mind paying some others, right?

For example, I doubt anyone is too grumpy about National Insurance payments being used to fund the NHS. If road tax was actually used to fix the potholes in our roads, we wouldn't particularly mind that either, would we? And, of course, we have to pay all those hamsters that run around in those wheels, creating electricity to power our homes. Those are Good Bills. The ones that power your home, pay for your broken leg to be fixed (sorry if you're reading this in America.[40] I genuinely am sorry for the U.S. Imagine having to choose between paying for your house or paying for your cancer treatment? Just, ugh) and pay for you to be allowed to turn on your tap every now and again.

But then there are the Rubbish Bills. The money you pay to the council, simply for the privilege of living in your house? That sucks. Paying half of your wages simply to be allowed to communicate with other beings? Also rubbish. Giving loads of your hard earned wonga to someone who is supposed to fix those holes

---

38 Or your wife/husband/significant other/children/pets can't .

39 Sign up for a year and the last spider is free.

40 I really do have delusions of grandeur, don't I? – *You do indeed, Miss Hancock. It is part of your charm.*

in the road that are the reason you have to keep replacing your tyres? That's a really irritating one.[41]

Sadly, we don't have any life hacks for this section. Unless you decide to give it all up and start an Amish community, using candles for lighting and gadding about in a horse and cart, you're pretty much stuck with paying bills until the day you die.[42] But we do give you express permission to be really grumpy about it, and to mutter ominous, pointless threats as you helplessly watch your money trickling right through your fingers.

---

[41]   Am I to understand that you have an automobile, Miss Hancock? I'm afraid that is one of the conveniences of modern life which has passed me by, along with the microwave oven and augmented reality. In what exciting times we live!

[42]   And even if you do this, you'll probably still have to fit into B and C while living in your hovel.

Love Life

This may just sound like some advice that is written on an inspirational poster or a pointless wall hanging ornament that your mate bought you for Christmas, but it is, in fact, something you have to cope with in life. It can be great, it can be awful, and both these can occur within the space of a few minutes, but it is something you are going to struggle to avoid. Unless you decide that life is actually better and easier without the added hassle of An Extra Being, in which case we would not blame you at all.

As we have all been told, by our beloved Disney, all we need to do in order to Live Happily Ever After is to meet The One, Fall In Love, and Skip Off Into The Sunset. (Too many capitals? I thought so too.)

As it turns out, real life is not so simple as all that.

Prince Charming snores. Cinderella has herpes. Aladdin is a compulsive liar. Snow White has literally no conversation. The list goes on.

As we age, we realise that there is pretty much no way we are going to meet The One and then everything else is going to fall into place. In order to have a healthy, meaningful relationship with another flawed human being, we have to accept our own flaws. And theirs. Or, you can just give it all up and get cats.[43]

Although it isn't really the be all and end all of everything, dating can be a fun thing to do – plus it beats sitting at home alone on Saturday nights. And you can pretend you're in an Attenborough documentary and narrate your evening – just try to ensure you do this in your head rather than out loud. Narrating a date in the style of Attenborough will probably result in not many more dates.[44]

We can't actually get away from wanting to Be With Someone, despite how cynical we become. This is because of the fact that all creatures on this earth are driven by a primeval instinct to procreate.[45] Although the technology is gearing up that will allow us to pretty much create life with just one person, this wouldn't be much fun, would it? Also, there is the thought of becoming an old person and sitting all on your own in your nursing home, with no other similarly ancient person there to laugh at your creaking joints and ruffle your bald head.

The world of love[46] is a tricky business. It is really, astonishingly hard to find someone who is even remotely compatible with you, despite the fact that there are literally billions of us. You can try the old fashioned way of wandering about until you bump into someone vaguely personable, or you can go down the modern route of dating apps – whichever way you do it, finding someone to co habit/procreate/enjoy life with is actually really tricky.

It may be that we are all destined, fated, written in the stars – whichever word you want to use for it – to find someone (or someones) to make our lives more pleasant, or it may just be a complete pile of randomness. Who knows. I certainly don't. If you figure it out, be sure to let me know.

This being said, there are a few hints and tips we can offer you when you are setting out into the world of getting into the world of other people's pants:

---

43 Do this. We should all do this, it's much less hassle. Although, see Pets – you're probably better off with rats.

44 But the ones you did have would be pretty ace.

45 Or at least practise.

46 Or just the stuff that goes with it, like the fun stuff.

Sex

Er. Excuse me. You appear to have not only put this in BEFORE the marriage section, but even before the dating and co-habiting. I assume this is some kind of error?

Actually, no. We know what we're talking about.

This is the first section that has to be included in anything that involves Relations with the Opposite Sex. Or the Same Sex. Whatever is your thing, you must always make sure that you test the goods before you sign on the dotted line.

Do not let anyone force you into any form of co-habiting, let alone marriage, before you have tested the goods. Some people simply aren't compatible when playing the sausage hiding game[47] and other people aren't very good at it, and I for one wouldn't want to find that out after a lifelong commitment. Hell, you wouldn't buy a car without taking a test drive first, then why do so with a prospective life partner?

In theory this is the only car you're going to be driving[48] for the rest of your life so don't wait until after you've purchased it to find out you can't get on with the gear stick, it conks out before you're even halfway to where you want to go, or you don't like its bumpers.

Oh, and if you do try it out and things are good, then do it as often as you, and said partner, want. It is the one 'sin' that is fun, free, good for you and does no harm to anyone else or to the planet.[49] Don't listen to what anyone else tells you.

Sex is one of those brilliant things that you can just DO, as a human being – you don't have to take any tests or pass any qualifications – you can just do it. In fact, this is how the human race has continued for so long. It's because people just do it, all the time.

And, it turns out, it's pretty good fun! Definitely beats sitting alone on the sofa watching re-runs of *Strictly*.[50] However, if you find yourself sitting on the sofa WITH company, turning down a roll in the hay in favour of watching *Strictly*, then maybe it's time to find yourself a better dance partner. If you know what I mean.

---

47 Under the sofa, again? Get some imagination. – *Some decorum, please, Miss Hancock! We mustn't frighten the horses.*

48 Unless you're lucky enough to be from before the 6th century. See Marriage.

49 Assuming you're sensible of course. Extra humans aren't necessarily what the planet needs right now.

50 *Anything is better than that, Miss Hancock.*

It really helps, in the bedroom[51] department, if you find someone who shares your, ahem, interests. It's no good shacking up with someone who likes to dress up in a gimp suit if you're allergic to latex, for example. And if you are claustrophobic, for goodness' sake ditch the one who is really into serious bondage.

But, once you've figured out the things you like and the things they like, go for your life! Sex is great, it should NEVER be taboo, and it is something that should be freely and joyfully enjoyed by all parties.[52] There is nothing shameful about enjoying your body and what it can do, in combination with someone else's body and what it can do.

The Victorians did a lot of damage, didn't they? As have a lot of the religions, by making us think that there was something wrong with doing what comes so naturally to us, and what is literally the only reason that humanity has got past the point of living in caves saying Ug, and have got to the point now where we can travel to space and dye our hair all the colours of the rainbow. There is nothing wrong with sex. Nothing at all – and in fact it really has a lot of things going for it as well as the inevitable reaction of producing new generations:

- It's fun. As long as you do it right, and find a partner who also does it right, there really are much worse ways to spend a Friday night. Along with dolphins, humanity is one of the only species that have sex for fun (probably because most other species haven't invented condoms), so let's live up to our reputation and get it on.

- It's good exercise. If you are looking to lose a pound or two but you hate jogging, go for a bit of bedroom acrobatics instead. You don't have to bring gymnastic equipment or swing from the lightshades, but a good session will definitely burn off that fancy chocolate brownie you sneaked in at lunchtime.

- It's good for the mental health. Sex releases dopamine and endorphins, so it is as good as a session at the gym for making you feel relaxed and happy. Better than the gym, in fact. If your gym makes you feel as good as sex does, then I definitely need to switch.

- It passes the time. If you're a bit bored of a weekend but you can't be bothered to go out, why not indulge in a bit of nookie instead? That way you can kid yourself that you're still young and exciting, and you haven't had to spend loads of money or put strain on your liver.

---

51   Sofa, garden, treehouse, Argos.
52   If you have THIS sort of party then do send me your address and we'll talk.

The one thing we really must include is: Consent. Both yours and someone else's. Both parties have got to be well up for it, otherwise it borders on the morally wrong and illegal, and is, in my opinion, a shootable offence. It's ok if you wanted it a while ago then changed your mind, or didn't want it but now you do. As long as you're honest with your fellow bed bouncer, all should be well. If they throw all their toys out of the pram at any point, pick up your gimp suit and flounce from the room, letting the door hit them in the face on your way out.

Dating

Ugh.

Yes, this is the first paragraph. Just ugh.

Anyone who's ever dated, whether in the traditional way of randomly meeting someone or doing it determinedly by joining one of the billion dating apps that promise you eternal happiness, will have made that noise at some point – probably more than once, and possibly even every single day.

Dating these days has made what's on the outside even more important. Online dating is a horrible place to be; somewhere that you can be judged and discarded within a millisecond, based merely on your photograph. Milliseconds to sum you up and decide you are not to someone's liking. At least in the olden days it would take a girl at least 5 minutes to realise that she really, really needed to nip home and wash her hair. With the success rate of my flirting, my local area must have had the shiniest and most nit free females in Europe. Nice to know I've done my part.[53]

People are all so busy now. Old-style dating takes too long, hence the prevalence of online dating apps. Nowadays you can do most of the groundwork over text messages whilst doing your shopping/ironing/pooing/sitting on the sofa with your current squeeze, and you only really need to meet up when both of you are convinced that the other is someone they'd probably like to get naked with. There are still some fundamental things the internet can't replace.

It turns out that finding The[54] One is much harder than skipping through a forest glade and swooning over some gorgeous tall beautiful stranger, who just happens to share all your interests and will help you to become a better version of yourself. No, dating these days is an absolute minefield.

---

53   It would be nicer if *they* had, though.

54   Next

Look at that profile picture; aren't they gorgeous? (But, are they secretly a troll who is sweating over your depressingly honest pictures, and sucking you in with ideas of how great they are because they've stalked your Facebook profile and learned your political preferences off by heart?)

That lovely person in the bar making eyes at you. Oh, they are perfect, surely! (But how do you know they don't have a vial of Rohypnol up their sleeve?)

What about that cutie that your friend introduced you to... Swoon! (Who knows that they're not actually a serial killer just desperate to add your face to their collection of frozen body parts?)

Your best bet, when dating, is to throw yourself into it and hope for the best. And also, tell EVERYONE where you're going on the first date, and make sure that you have a couple of good friends primed to phone you up with an 'emergency' at the drop of a text as you hide your phone beneath the table, glassy eyed from trying to smile with feigned interest as Geoffrey insists on listing the entire collection of his very expensive wine cellar.

Here are a few common pitfalls, plus a fun little quiz (who doesn't love a quiz?) to see you through some common issues in the early days of dating:

(1)

Everyone farts. You have been invited back to your date's place for the first time, when you feel the telltale rumblings. What do you do?

  (a) Run from the building, shouting over your shoulder that you have a family emergency. Fart with great relief after you have made it less than 100 yards, then do the Walk Of Shame from the building and ghost that date for the rest of time.

  (b) Lift a leg shamelessly and waft the smell towards your date. After all, if you marry them they're stuck with this for the rest of time, right?

  (c) Clamp your buttcheeks shut and waddle uncomfortably around the place, also keeping your lips clamped shut in case it decides to escape from the other end. Get ghosted by your date for being totally uncommunicative, and frankly, a bit weird.

  (d) **Secret option:** Sweep over to the window, exclaiming loudly, 'Oh! The moon is beautiful tonight!' Lift one buttcheek away from the other and fart silently and triumphantly, then sweep away from the area just as your beloved tries to follow you. Blame the resulting smell on the dog, or, if there is no dog, gaslight[55] said beloved into thinking that actually THEY farted and you are horrified at their actions.[56]

Or…

Realise that we are all people. Actually, we are all mammals; working objects that process food and deal with bodily issues. Things actually get better and more comfortable (both physically and mentally) when you start to talk about poo. Try it! I bet there isn't a single friend in your group who has not had digestive issues, or isn't currently enjoying digestive issues bubbling through them.

Nothing about our bodies should be taboo. Talk about all the stuff. Chances are you will release a tidal wave of joy and relief, as people realise that YOU are the person that can make them feel normal!

Did you hear the story of the woman who literally climbed out of the bathroom window because she had gone to the toilet in her date's house and it wouldn't flush? Yes, it would be embarrassing to face your crush with the news that you left a log the size of a Californian Redwood in their toilet, and they're now going to have to call a plumber or unbend a coat hanger and get deep into the U-bend – but what if you were just honest about it, ended up marrying the person and had a hilarious tale to make the grandchildren cringe with?[57]

(2)

You are excitedly on the way to the bedroom for the first time with your delightful, swoony date. On a brief tryst by their bookshelf, you spot a copy of *50 Shades Of Grey*. What do you do?

(a) Whip out your latex bodysuit and unfold your telescopic cat o' nine tails, flexing your muscles threateningly as you don your gimp mask and fasten a gag around your date's mouth.

(b) Instantly remove yourself from the building in whatever clothes you are still currently wearing, screaming over your shoulder that you only wanted a bit of Missionary and a post coital fag. Spend the next 9 hours in the pub with your mates, bemoaning the fact that They Really Are All Bastards.

---

55   Considering what you have just dropped, gaslighting seems a dangerous and possibly explosive approach.

56   *This adolescent obsession with farting is rather tedious, Miss Hancock.*

57   Actually, this is my preferred method of dealing with life. If you've met me, you'll understand.

(c) Postpone the shag session for a trip to the local charity shop, the one who had so many copies of this book donated that they made a fort for people to sit and read it in before they flung it away with disgust. Loudly discuss the fact that your main issue is not the subject material, but the truly appalling writing.

(d) **Secret option:** Carry on as you were. When it gets to the crunch, as it were, realise that the best thing you can do with any potential new bed buddy is to try things out, go with the flow, and gently tell them what you like and don't like. It'll probably turn out that the book was a stupid gift from some hilarious colleague as a Secret Santa gift.

The thing is, when it comes to Doing The Deed, everyone has things that they like and don't like. Nothing is off the table (in fact sometimes the table is the best place), so you can pretty much make it clear what you like and be relatively sure that at some point it will be done to you. Luckily, most people enjoy giving pleasure as much as they enjoy receiving it (masochists are, obviously, the exception) so as long as your thing isn't being dangled upside down in a large vat of jelly before being smothered with hungry maggots, you are pretty much guaranteed to find someone who will enjoy it with you. Actually, the jelly thing probably exists too.

(3)

You're meeting the parents for the first time?[58] Huge congratulations! Obviously, you want to make the best first impression. So what do you do?

(a) Fling your arms around your new in laws, enveloping them in not only your love and adoration, but also your nervous sweat. Watch your lover cringe as you embrace his mother, he having forgotten to mention to you that she has an aversion to physical contact.

(b) Walk into their house as if you own it, sniffing as you pass the beloved family photos, and sitting aloof as you are introduced to Aunt Ethel. Yes, she has false teeth, yes she removes them at dinnertime and sucks the life out of her food, yes you should simply avert your eyes and slurp your soup loudly to drown out the sound of Ethel. Choose to loudly 'tut' and make fake gagging noises instead.

---

[58] Theirs, that is. If it's your parents you are meeting for the first time then this is a very different scenario.

(c) Sit frozen and terrified as you are handed around like a prize antique. Listen in astonishment as lies about your family and their connections pass your lips. Wish for the ground to swallow you up.

(d) **Secret option:** Be yourself. If the person whose parents it is has seen fit to introduce you to the beings that made them, then surely you are worthy enough to act as your whole, entire, unadulterated self. Even if you are a total freak, the parents will be so thrilled that their hideous offspring has found a love interest that you will be welcomed into the family fold. Just maybe keep your secret hobby of taxidermy under wraps for the very first meeting.

Co-Habitation

So, you've made your way through the minefield that is dating, and you've found yourself a Not-Too-Hideous human being who you are willing to give up space in your Best Knicker Drawer for. Woohoo! Go you, I'm thrilled!

However, you should – especially if this is your first foray into starry eyed Living Together bliss – take heed. Go into this with your eyes open, and you should end up with the best of situations: someone with whom you can enjoy spending time, and who puts up with your disgusting habits because you put up with theirs, so you only ever have minor disagreements such as whose turn it is to put out the bins and who should clear up the biscuit crumbs in the bed.

If you're lucky, you will find a decent human being to shack up with; one that shares your hobbies and interests and doesn't mind the dog sleeping in the bed. The ideal home sharing human will be:

Willing to work incredibly hard to keep the home clean

Happy to do your fair share of cooking as well as theirs

Ever ready with the takeaway menus

An expert at running the perfect bubble bath

Really keen on giving back/neck/foot massages

Rich

Beautiful

If none of these things apply to your chosen housemate, then you should at least hope that they share some of your interests – or stay out of them completely.[59]

It turns out that sharing your precious space with another human can actually be really hard. Some people are easy, and will instantly morph into the perfect being – but chances are they will morph out of it quite soon after the honeymoon period wears off, and you will be left with someone who, it turns out is actually just a human being. With you also being an actual human being, this can cause a wee bit of friction.

As always, the best thing you can do is sit down, talk about how you are feeling and be honest about your expectations.[60] If your co-habitee doesn't KNOW that you demand at least 6 hours a week in total silence to meditate and communicate with higher beings, you can't really blame them for playing thrash metal at full volume every day. Tell them before you move in together that you get night terrors and they may regularly wake up to see you crawling on the ceiling like a scene from the Exorcist, then they'll be less likely to run screaming from the house the first time it happens. If you have a penchant for playing the bagpipes, do let them know[61] before they unpack their bags.

Also, you unfortunately have to listen to and accept their various demands of living together too. If you can accept their hideous habits, you stand half a chance of them accepting yours, and you might just muddle along quite happily.[62]

Marriage

This is actually a pretty outdated situation, if you think about it. Marriage began as a way to tell the world that you have chosen one particular person to be shackled to for the rest of time – but it didn't use to be the massive money-spinning festival that it is in this day and age.

Marriage has, almost certainly, been around since the beginning of humanity. However, the earliest recorded marriage took place around 2350 BC, in the far east. Who knew? Initially, marriage involved several partners, usually more females than males (hands up who is less than surprised by this fact?) Monogamy was not

---

[59]   Stay out of your hobbies, or out of your person?

[60]   With the exception of having a chat with, say, Boris Johnson. This will do no good, and will only piss you off.

[61]   And you will probably be saved the horrors of ever living with anyone. Ever. *Come, come, Miss Hancock! The melodic skirl of the pipes promotes conjugal harmony.*

[62]   Or at least, not too miserable for at least 50% of the time.

the main idea behind marriage until sometime between the 6th and 9th centuries (this is why we call these the Spoilsport Centuries).

Marriage was often conducted as a method of joining families together, for political gain or preventing wars. In many cases, particularly for noble aristocratic houses, the couples involved would have no say in the matter, and they could be married at shockingly young ages. Some cultures these days still practise arranged marriages, and although in some cases it can be pretty successful, most people are moving away from the idea of being forced to marry someone they have, in many cases, not even met. This is definitely the right direction in which to be heading.

Let's face it though, the main reason for getting married was to get into your crush's pants, right? Apparently, any extra-marital activity would cause great rage and fury to Him Upstairs ('cos he only likes virgins, as we know) and the offending couple would be smitten, denied a place in heaven – or worse, be left with a child. The horror!

These days, marriage seems to be more of an excuse for a gigantic knees-up than any of the above reasons, and everyone swapping their blood for alcohol. And, it doesn't even last that long! In some cases, the hangover from the wedding goes on longer than the marriage itself. Which brings us to the D-Word...

In Native American cultures, it is widely rumoured that a woman could divorce a man by simply leaving his moccasins outside the teepee. This sounds far cheaper and less hassle than going through a court case to divorce your unfaithful ex, doesn't it?

Divorcing someone for any reason is needlessly difficult. It really should be as simple as,

'Please, yer Honour, I just don't like him any more. He snores, he doesn't like Aunt Ethel, and he NEVER puts the bins out.'

But, ohhh no. You will have to jump through a million and one hoops, including stating why you want to divorce (surely, not loving someone any more is the best reason to not be shackled to them for the rest of time? This is the stuff murders are made from) and then paying out a sizeable chunk of your hard earned earnings – and that's just the simple kind, that doesn't involve kids, finances, housing or any of the other things that complicate life in the first place!

In my humble opinion, it makes far more sense to live with someone for as long as is mutually acceptable; have the massive party without the legally binding contract, and keep your finances strictly separate. Unfortunately this is not possible with kids – but it actually is with housing.

I once knew a guy who had been in a happy, fulfilling relationship for almost 20 years – the secret to this longevity is, probably, the fact that they never lived together. Each would spend a few nights a week at the other's house, then return to their own comfortable abode, breathe a sigh of relief and spend the entire evening farting, scratching and deliberately leaving toenail clippings on the table.

Unfortunately, this is not actually the best story to showcase a successful relationship, because ultimately it ended. He cheated on her. At 78. And that's all I have to say about that.

But anyway, it seems to me that maintaining oneself in a relationship is very important, or you run the risk of being one of those couples who eventually morph into one another. You know the ones; they buy matching lycra onesies because one of them likes cycling, and both give up flour because one of them is intolerant to gluten. They use the phrase 'We' when discussing themselves, and probably have a soppy picture of their partner on their phone. Eventually, you will be very confused when you invite your friend over, to be faced with a half-man half-woman hybrid, who calls herself 'Jennifer Brown-Was-Freestone' on Facebook, just in case there was anyone who knew them before they became one half of a very strange couple.

Oh, and another thing! 'My other half' is a phrase that sends shivers of rage up and down my whole body. Seriously, is it ok to say that we are not a whole person without being attached to another? What happened to freedom, independence, the love of one's life before having found another member of the human race to physically and mentally attach oneself to? What happened to our pride, or sense of self, our fierce independence, god dammit?

Ok, I admit – I do possibly bang on about this a little too much. But seriously, we would all be much happier if we realised that true happiness comes from ourselves, not another person.

How huge a responsibility is is to be lumbered with the expectation that YOU, and YOU ALONE are responsible for making another person happy? Be honest, you can't even make yourself happy, can you? Maybe it would be best to start with that before you go foisting yourself upon another unwary human.

Splitting Up

Splitting up, despite the fact that we have all been taught that this is the anathema we must avoid even more carefully than Herpes, actually does happen.[63] In fact,

---

[63] Often due to the aforementioned Herpes.

it happens more often than staying together. *Collective gasp* I know! It's like it's… Normal, or something! Humour me for a moment.

Count on your hands the number of successful relationships you've had. I've got a bit of time; I'll wait while you work out the maths.

Done it? Ok. Chances are, if you're one of the lucky ones, you have ONE relationship that has not fallen apart. You are probably still in it, otherwise it would join the pile of failed ones that you spent so long counting back there, and you would have come up with the answer far more quickly.

Congrats on your successful relationship! I'm genuinely happy for you and your significant other; long may it continue.[64]

If you fall into the (possibly slightly larger) category of those who have yet to find The One, or those who found The One and discovered they were anything but, I have a little bit of advice for you:

It

        is

                OK

                        to

                                split

                                        up

I thought I'd lay it out for you, because so often we feel like we're letting the entire world down if we decide that Gaz the failed rap artist, or Chereese the aspiring masseuse, aren't actually the people we want to marry.

I read a fantastic article recently, called 'Why do people keep trying (and failing) at monogamy?' The answer to this is that actually, we're not really cut out for it, from both an evolutionary and social way. We kind of keep doing it (emphasis on the 'kind of') but none of our hearts are particularly in it.

It turns out that the world doesn't actually end when your relationships do.[65] There may be wailing and gnashing of teeth, and sometimes a real, true, serious heartbreak that can go on for years.

I know this. You know this. We've all been there. (A moment's silence for that…)

Then, yeeeeaaaahhhhhh, life gets loads better all of a sudden! It turns out that you didn't have to put up with that great big snoring lump, or finding toenail

---

[64] Unless you get miserable, in which case I wish you speedy freedom.

[65] Although it does feel like it at the time, doesn't it? But the world actually ending would involve far fewer plates being thrown – that's how you'll know the difference.

clippings in the bed, or snapping at them every time they did that thing that pissed you off that you'd told them about A MILLION TIMES yet they still kept doing it! Who knew?

Ok, there may be days, weeks, months or even years of feeling sad about it... But then oh my goodness, the freedom! Life carries on! Nobody died![66]

Sometimes you may lose a social circle or two, and this can be really sad. But everybody has their teams to support, and even if the people you thought were friends now have to be Team Ex, this is fine. Don't write them tear stained letters or turn up at their houses begging for an audience. They are probably as upset as you – but we all have to have some morals and loyalties somewhere.[67]

It is highly recommended, when you do split up with someone, that you do not obsessively stalk them. Unfortunately, stalking is much easier to do in this day and age, with Facebook, travel and mobile phones – in the old days, all you had to do was end the relationship then skip off to sea on a pirate galleon, or move two miles to the next village, safe in the knowledge that your ex didn't own a horse and so could not lurk outside your windows at night.

Another thing you should try to avoid is parading your new found happiness in front of your ex like a young Labrador showing you its toy. They may have taken it worse than you, or even taken it better – but still, there's no need to be a dick. When you get into a relationship with someone, chances are there are reasons behind this -whether a fiery physical attraction, a delicious mental connection, or a combination of the two. Or, maybe you were just the last two people by the bar on a Friday night and someone (you will argue for the rest of time over who said it. In fact, maybe this is why you split up in the first place?) drunkenly slurred, 'Fancy a shag?'

Whatever the reason that you shared your body and your soul with this person, there was a connection between you. This is something that should be respected, and the memory of them treated with kindness – once you've got over the initial he said/she said/they said/you're an arse who ruined my life bit, of course.

---

[66] If this was the reason for the relationship ending, then I am truly, truly sorry for being a heartless bastard. I only included this for the laughs. On the other hand, if the relationship ended because you were the cause of somebody dying, then go and turn yourself in right now. Seriously. We're pretty easygoing, but we don't condone murder. Even if they snored.

[67] Maybe your ex will treat them as badly as they treated you in the future, then you can form an I HATE THEM CLUB in a few months?

Parenthood

Apparently, this is the reason that we are all here. In fact, if this were not the reason that we were all here, then the vast majority of us would not be here.[68]

You may be the sort of person who has longed for parenthood since you became aware that there were other people in the world besides you.

---

[68] Although, accidents do happen.

You may be a person who has had parenthood sprung upon them like a toddler leaping out from behind a sofa – whether that be your own offspring or being saddled with someone else's.

Or, you may be someone who views the idea of reproducing with the same joy as, say, the idea of a nuclear holocaust.[69]

Whatever your views on kids, they will be present in your life. They may be your own; they may be your friends' or family's; or they may be those irritating little wasps that swarm around you during peaceful afternoons at the pub, making you feel unsure how the human race has ever survived this long, because let's face it – kids you're not related to are pretty grim. In fairness, I bet some of the ones you ARE related to are a bit rubbish, too. Maybe the key is that pubs didn't exist in Neanderthal times...

Bearing in mind that infanticide is, at best, frowned upon, dealing with children in some way is definitely going to be a part of your life. We no longer live in Victorian times where they can be placated with a pat on the head and a 'See you when you grow up.'

So, unfortunately, you're going to have to deal with them one way or another.

To Breed Or Not To Breed?

Especially in this day and age, many people may feel stuck between a rock and a hard place when it comes to continuing the human race. On the one hand, creating adorable little copies of yourself and your beloved partner is a rosy tinted dream that many of us harbour;[70] while on the other hand, who wants to bring new, innocent life into this shitstorm that we have created?

Fears about body changes, the birth itself, and the following period of newborn craziness, plus the worries about responsibly taking care of another entire human, are well founded and should be seriously thought about.

Plus, there is the absolutely bone chilling, soul wrenching thought that should put any potential parent off, even more than The Omen does... What if your kids turn into Tory voters?

There are also a lot of advantages to not having kids. The lie-ins! The productivity![71] The cleanliness of your house!

But...

---

[69] Let's face it, there will probably be the same amount of vomit and carnage.
[70] Adorableness not guaranteed.
[71] Why, oh why did I not write books before I had a child?!?

They're actually pretty fab. In between all the poo, the tantrums, the snot (seriously, do these guys mine it or something?) and the constant

'Whyyyyy, Mummy?'

Kids are just the most heart-meltingly, world-changingly, utterly totally wonderful miniature human beings... Especially your own.

When you have children, you will suddenly develop a sneering disregard for other peoples', even the ones that you previously adored. Yes, little Tarquin may be a virtuoso violinist, and wee Clarissa will sit smiling her dimpled smile all day, while your own rugrats spend their time eating toilet roll and wiping bogies on the walls – but there is nothing like the spawn of your own blood to make you dissolve into a pile of parental adoration.

So, you've decided[72] to reproduce. Awesome, congratulations! You've decided not to? Awesome, congratulations!

This should, in all honesty, be the start and the end of the conversation. However, it is at this point that you will discover that everyone, EVERYONE, from the bin man to Aunt Ethel, now has an opinion on your ovaries:

- **Babies** Aren't you a bit too old?

- **No babies** But, are you SURE you don't want them?

- **Babies** Aren't you a bit too young?

- **No babies** What happens if you regret your decision when you're old?[73]

- **Babies** Are you eating enough veggies?

- **No babies** Maybe you just haven't met the right person?

- **Babies** Have you quit smoking?

- **No babies** What if not having kids make you take irresponsible life choices?

- **Babies** How are you going to afford them?

- **No babies** What are you going to do with all your excess money?

- **Babies** What if something goes wrong (insert story of some random unknown who had some medical issue that you have never heard of but that will keep you up at night for the next ten years).

---

72 Or not decided and had it sprung on you – no one's judging here.
73 To be fair, this can be applied to either decision.

- **No babies** Are you trying hard enough?

- **Babies** Have you tried lying on your back with your legs pointing at Mecca while chanting the alphabet backwards in Hebrew?

And God, don't even get me started on when you're actually pregnant... Since when is it ok to walk up to a stranger and start rubbing their stomach in broad daylight?[74] I have a friend to whom it happened to so much she wanted to get a t-shirt printed that said: 'It's not a fucking lamp! A genie will not fucking pop out if you keep rubbing it!'

I think she could have made millions. But then she had a baby and had no time. Ever again.

Everyone will have an opinion on your due date and how many you're carrying, from your actual professional gynaecologist to your actual random stranger on the street. You might want to consider carrying a placard around with you, stating the due date, the sex, whether or not it's multiples, and whether or not you welcome the opinion of every single stranger who gleefully notices your condition and decides to weigh in with their six eggs.

Also, what's the deal with that knowing little wink and asking about 'Number Two?' Yes, sometimes this even happens while you're pregnant with Number One. If you're lucky, they'll wait at least until your stitches have healed before they start. If not, they'll be there in the hospital, leaning over you with that knowing wink, making you feel like a breeding sow.

I always felt like screaming, 'If I can ever wash the shit off me for long enough to smell half human, and if I'd slept more than 3 hours in the whole of last month, and if I can EVER burn the smell of baby sick from the inside of my nostrils, then I will consider it! But for right now, my partner and his useless nipples sleep on the sofa, and the only interaction we have in the day is when we wordlessly pass each other the child in a grotesque parody of 'Pass the screaming parcel!''

Most people scuttled away, terrified (or, more likely, repulsed by the smell of baby sick and my Medusa hair, unwashed for months and filled with the aforementioned baby sick).

Babies

Oh. My. God. Babies...

---

[74] I think doing this in pitch darkness may be even worse.

They're cute, adorable, world shaking and utterly wonderful. But, aren't these little miniature versions of ourselves utterly TERRIFYING?!

Think about it. You have to take tests every day throughout life, to make sure you are ready for the next step. SATS! Exams! Driving tests! Interviews!

But, if you want to reproduce; to create the next glorious stage of humanity's existence – you can literally do this without anyone checking that you are in a mental and physical state to do so.

No one questions your ability to reproduce. No one at all.[75] There is no one that will check your genetics, or your criminal record, or your GCSE results. Anyone, ANYONE is allowed to create the Next Generation.

I remember approaching the desk in my local GP, clutching my positive pregnancy test,[76] trembling slightly. I nervously told them my diagnosis: 'I am incubating a small human!'

I was astounded by the response. There were no banners. There were no balloons.

No one leapt from behind the counter, shouting congratulations and showering me with confetti and singing my praises for helping to continue the human race.

No, I was met with a half-hearted smile and a wave of the hand from the receptionist,[77] a fumble under the desk[78] to pass me a pile of leaflets, and an admonition to return at 12 weeks 'when the pregnancy is viable'.

Oh, my heart. And then, oh, my head! How is it OK to just release people into the world, knowing they're potentially carrying a small bunch of cells that will turn into a whole person, and leaving them to it for the next 3 months? What if I was to develop an addiction to skydiving? What if my cravings led me directly to the doorway of raw meat and fish and blue cheese? What if I inadvertently became a 70 a day smoker?[79]

How is it ok to just leave people alone with potentially the biggest news of their lives, especially knowing how rubbish most of us are? I'm assuming that doctors believe that this method is a 'weed out the weak' strategy.

- Babies are hard work. Hang on, let me rephrase – babies are Hard Work. There are a few things you should know before you have one:

---

75 This statement does not include the Mother-in-Law.

76 Not literally. You only go into a doctor's holding wee if you suspect a UTI. Unless you're some kind of weirdo.

77 What is *with* GP receptionists? They're all arseholes! *Come, come Miss Hancock! They have a difficult job and most of them do it well.*

78 Is this how the pregnancy happened too? Not judging.

79 I was close to this, to be fair – closer after seeing those two little lines.

- They never sleep. Babies are genetically programmed for survival. This means they will wake up every two hours[80] looking for food. No amount of sleep training, switching to formula or weaning onto food early will prevent this constant disturbing of your sleep.

- They are completely useless. Because of the size of humans' brains, our offspring have to be born at least 4 months early. If they incubated any longer, their massive heads would literally not fit out of us. This is a pretty huge design flaw, especially when you compare us to gazelles, who are leaping about the plains hours after popping out.

- They are idiots, determined not to survive. Babies will put ANYTHING in their mouths, from dog poo to poisonous plants to Aunt Ethel's false teeth. In order to keep them alive, you have to teach them to not put stuff in their mouths while at the same time encouraging them to put stuff in their mouths that is good for them. Without fail, they will choose the former over the latter.

- They generally resemble anyone other than the person who has incubated them for 9 months and feeds them using their own bodily fluids. This is a sad thing for those of us who did the incubating; but at least you can comfort yourself that they won't end up with your chin.

The thing is, as soon as you have a baby, you are opening yourself up to judgement from every corner of society.

Are you breastfeeding? Ohhh, shock horror! This will provide your child with an attachment disorder for the rest of time! Are you sure you're not doing it just for you?[81]

- Are you bottle feeding? Ohhh, the horror! Did you not know this can cause your child multiple health issues throughout the rest of time? How could you be so irresponsible?[82]

- Cloth nappies, you say? Well that's lovely. But how about the risk of bacteria entering your precious child's private parts? And how can you possibly expect to keep that many nappies clean?

---

[80] If you're lucky.

[81] No. Just no. Anyone who has ever breastfed a baby knows that it is never, EVER for your own benefit. The cracked and bleeding nipples? Lovely! Just what I wanted! Mastitis? Oooh, fantastic – I love antibiotics and feeling like I'm about to die! The judgemental comments? These really make my day better!

[82] Keeping your child alive is not irresponsible, just so you know.

- You're using disposable nappies? Surely you know that they are clearly the work of the devil. How can you possibly expect to continue living on this planet when you are placing nappies that take 500 years to decompose into a landfill?[83]

- Are you weaning your child into lovingly prepared purées of various vegetable designed to help them become strong and healthy? Bah, what an awful human being! Didn't you know they will never develop a chewing reflex if you do this?

- If you're considering Baby-Led Weaning, do let me send you literature on the number of babies who have choked to death on those semi-chilled sticks of death… How could you!

- Have you considered homeschooling? No? What a terrible parent you are! How could you not want your child with you every single second of every single day!

- Are you sending them to school? Oooh, just imagine what horrors they will come home from school with![84] You're clearly an irresponsible parent!

And, the worst thing is that many of these comments come from people who don't even HAVE kids. Or people who did have them decades ago, when it was considered fine and normal to smoke and drink your way through pregnancy, and leave your child outside in a pram in the middle of November because 'the fresh air is good for them'.

It's almost as bad when the comments come from other parents, because then you get to fill yourself with self doubt – what if they actually ARE right, and you really are just a terrible parent? I mean, their Facebook account is filled with sunny, smiling babies and happy, refreshed looking parents.[85]

The thing to remember is… Everyone has an opinion about your life. Until you have a baby though, they tend to have the courtesy to only voice those opinions when your back is turned and you have no chance to defend yourself. As soon as your little Mini Me pops out, off come the gloves.

---

83 Actually, we're right there with this one. We'll look into the stats if you're interested. But seriously. Reusable nappies are the way forward. We'll leave it there for now because we don't mean to nag, but still…

84 To be fair, they bring hideous, hideous diseases home from school. Boil your hands after every time you touch them.

85 Pro tip: turn up on their doorstep when they are not expecting you and cannot hide behind filters and phone apps and soppy 'Live Love Laugh' signs. They'll be wiping snot, clearing up poo and screaming into pillows with the best of us.

When it comes to your kids, you and YOU ALONE know what is right. It's fine to ask for help and opinions, obviously, and it's fine to run home screaming to Mum's once in a while for a good sob.[86]

It is not fine to base your entire parenting strategy on the overly helpful[87] advice from Aunt Ethel, the bin man, or various friends and family who are trying to make you into clones of themselves, and turn your kids into screaming horrors just like theirs are or were.

Develop a few coping strategies, like:

- Smiling glassily over their shoulder and suddenly pointing out that they appear to have left the house without their underwear.

- Answering their advice in interpretative dance.

- Offering to bring the baby round to their for the afternoon while you go to the spa.

- Aiming a particularly offensively snotty child in their direction and sprinkling pepper around.

- Politely but firmly saying, 'Thanks for your advice! We're going to do what works for us, but we appreciate your input.'

Toddlers

Ahhh, these guys. Forget the newborn haze and the lack of sleep and being covered with another human's bodily fluids day in and day out – toddlers are the ones that make your hair prematurely grey and have you wistfully eyeing up the gin bottle at 10 a.m.

Toddlers are also commonly known as:

- Devil Spawn

- That Little Shit

- I'm Not Sure It's Even Mine

- Who Peed On The Carpet, Again?

---

86   She lives 250 miles away. You can also just call her.
87   Not helpful.

You know that little twinkle in the eyes of an old person, when they catch sight of your nearly-crawling baby, and they say, 'Ahh, you'll have your hands full soon!'

We laugh happily, picturing days chasing little Daisy as she scampers down mountain slopes, or guiding wee Magnus on his first forays into navigating a tricycle.

What we don't see is said Old Person returning to their quiet, peaceful, clean home, snickering into their hands as they picture the nightmares that are about to enter your life.

The thing with toddlers is, they are becoming People. And People, as we all know, have Opinions. However, most people can manage to keep their opinions to themselves (see Babies) and if they can't, you just don't have to be around them.

However, now you have your very own walking talking[88] human being, that you spawned from your very own cells, you have no choice but to be around them all the time. And, because you are around them all the time, and you are their safe haven – the one human who is designed to love them for all of time no matter what horrific thing they do – they tend to save their most horrific things just for you. Ain't that sweet?![89]

Toddlers are the reason that parents look haggard, grey and despairing. Next time you judge someone for screeching at their toddler, imagine what sort of day they have had up until that point. Then, take a vow of celibacy and live in the mountains for the rest of time, just so you won't be tempted to have one.

Although, there are a lot of great things about a toddler, don't get me wrong. Generally they start to talk, or at least make intelligible grunts, so their doting parents can understand them even if the rest of the world just hears gibberish. Their personalities start to develop, and they begin to show their preferences for things[90] and various different abilities. You can literally watch an entirely new being start to grow and blossom before your very eyes. It's miraculous! It's joyful! It brings tears of pride to the corners of your eyeballs! However.

Do they REALLY have to be such arseholes about it?!?

The tantrums. Ohhhh, the tantrums.

Woebetide you if you dare to prepare their favourite meal on the wrong plate.

---

[88] Neither of these things are guaranteed by toddler age, just so you know.
[89] It's fine to be rocking in the corner at this stage, by the way. I definitely am.
[90] Generally, all the things that you would prefer them not to prefer.

If you suggest that they walk about the length of their own bodies.

If you refuse to carry one more leaf/rock/manky bird feather home from the walk.

If you dare to suggest a different story before bedtime.

If... The list goes on.

If you took toddler behaviour and suggested to the world that it originated from Korea,[91] no one would be much surprised. However, in a civilised world, you are supposed to have your offspring well and truly under control and able to smile politely, sit quietly, use cutlery and the toilet, and not bark at random strangers by the age of four.

It's amazing, given how much of humanity has children, that people are so offended at the complete lack of socially acceptable behaviour.

The best thing that you can do with yours, assuming that you are doing your best to feed it, love it and keep it healthy, is to ignore anything that anyone tells you.

There are no 40-year-olds who still throw themselves to the floor, kicking and screaming, because they have not been allowed to buy their favourite treat. I know there's the obvious joke here – but Donald Trump is over 40, so we can't make this about him.

It is very rare to see a grown adult folding their arms, stomping their feet and refusing to eat, just because the meal was not served on their favourite plate.

You won't often see a 20 year old biting his best friend because said friend was having a lend of his favourite toy.[92]

Remember that we are all people. We are all different. We all have our likes and dislikes, and we all enjoy being treated with respect and courtesy. Give your toddler the same kindness – let them wear a pink tutu and Doc Martens if that's what makes them feel like they're expressing themselves! Let them help to cut their sandwich in just the right way (maybe then they'll realise how difficult it is, and give you less of a hard time).[93] Allow them a bit of autonomy, and maybe they will reward you by not growing up to be psychopaths.[94]

---

[91] What is this about Korea, Miss Hancock? The land which gave the world moveable metal type and, I believe, the first iron-clad ship, cannot be held responsible for the behaviour of British toddlers.

[92] That he hasn't played with for weeks, and only wants because Someone Else is holding it.

[93] HAHAHAHAHAAA. They won't do this. They'll just ruin your entire loaf, then STILL demand that you cut it into stars, or Peppa Pig's face

[94] This is not guaranteed.

Tweens

So, you've got them through the perils of babyhood with your sanity still mostly intact, then you navigated the pitfalls of toddlerhood and managed to prevent them eating poisonous mushrooms or choking on a grape. Chances are they go to school now, and are being coached to be relatively decent human beings. You assume that, now the really scary moments of babyness are past, and you have a few years before they turn into awful, smelly, lumbering teenagers, that you can have a little breather. Guess what? You're wrong.

Enter the Tween. This cutesey little word describes a child who is between childhood and teenagerhood, with an emphasis on the 'teen' bit. Get it? Cute and funny, right? Erm, na, not so much.

You see, these little creatures are evolving, once again, before your very eyes. They are now no longer babies, but they'll still hold your hand in public and sometimes have screaming meltdowns. They have Thoughts, Feelings and Opinions, but they are often not quite able to elucidate them very well. They are growing up and changing, and their poor little minds are as confused as their bodies are.

Yours probably is too. Why is little Jemima slamming doors, pouting and throwing her Barbies out of the window because you told her that 7 is too young to have her ears pierced? How come Magnus is already starting to smell like a hamster and spend inordinate amounts of time in his room? Surely you've got a few years of grace when they're still your little babies before the hormones start to kick in?

Puberty does appear to be starting earlier these days, so you are going to have to start slipping deodorants and shaving kits in their Christmas stockings sooner than you would have thought. Still, there will be some days when they are so adorably cute and snuggly that you feel like you're really winning at this parenting malarkey, and you can nostalgically remember them as small, cute bundles of cuteness. Just don't forget to take a photo to immortalise this, because it won't last.

Teenagers

I probably don't need to devote an entire chapter to these guys, do I? I mean, we've all been them, so we all know how obnoxious they are. But, they're a part of life -whether your own spawn or part of the gang of Yoof who hang around by the bus stop, intimidating old ladies.

You've had kids, and managed to keep them alive! Woop! Well done you; your reward for that servitude is the presence of teenagers! Wait, did I say reward? That may not be quite the right word.

You may remember being a teenager, when you were totally aware that you were God's Gift, and it was everyone else who was a terrible human being who didn't understand you, right?

You can understand behaviour like tantrums, door slamming and the excessive smell of an unwashed body – you remember Toddlers. Toddlers have very little choice over any of these things. However, teenagers are nearly adults, aren't they? They really should have a modicum of manners and the ability to clean themselves, shouldn't they?

The thing with teenagers is that their brains are literally not finished. The prefrontal cortex, the bit that is concerned with other people and doesn't believe that the entire universe revolves around oneself, doesn't completely finish linking up with the rest of the brain until around the mid 20s mark. While it may seem like in some people this achievement is never actually achieved, it may just be that they are arseholes.

You see, these things are big, and clever and opinionated and nearly grown up, and yet, unfortunately, STILL IN YOUR HOUSE. You are no longer sharing your home with children over whom you can reign supreme, but with almost-grown-ups with whom you must share mutual respect. This is difficult when the other human makes Ug noises that rival cave people, sleeps till midday, eats everything in your house and brings home prospective partners that make Hannibal Lecter look angelic.

There are good times, obviously, and some weeks these may outweigh the bad – but generally times with teenagers are tough times. But, the thing is, as they're getting older so are you, and they're beginning to realise that that they will be the ones choosing your nursing home, so you've kinda gotta continue being nice to them for the foreseeable.

And, these days this foreseeable stage is extended. The ridiculousness of the prices of housing mean that your kids are unlikely to ever able to move out until you've died so they can sell your house. This means that the teenage years are now extended into their late 20s,[95] and your misery extends pretty much into retirement.

The majority of teenagers have just a few simple requirements: food, sex and technology. A few might also require vast amounts of weed or bottles of cheap

---

[95]   If it's a boy one, mid 30s. They ain't going anywhere without a swift boot up the bottom.

cider in order to function, but the first three are pretty much all you need to keep your teenager happy.

- Without food they turn into a bear who has spotted a family of picnickers just before they go into hibernation. You may wish to consider getting a lock on your fridge, or at least hiding the crisp stash.

- Without sex, all those rampant newly formed hormones will be sprayed all over your walls and your teen will make Victor Meldrew look like a ray of sunshine. I'm not saying you should encourage underage sex, but if it helps your moody child-in-an-adult's-body less unbearable, then buy them a variety pack of condoms and send them on their way.

- Without technology they literally cannot function. Can you imagine today's teenagers actually having to talk to their friends face to face? Or get involved in an activity that didn't involve blowing things up or shooting things? God knows what will happen to these guys if/when society collapses and the WiFi goes down for good.

So, survival tips:

1. Stay calm. It's a tough time for them. Be the adult. If you can do this all the time then it's probably a good idea and will help to maintain harmony in your household. Unfortunately, this is impossible. Just try to minimise the shouting, even if they've left the light on in the bathroom for the hundredth time and when you headed to the stairs to inform them you tripped over their shoes.

2. Don't let them get hungry. Hungry people are grumpy people. Make sure there's plenty of snacks in the house. Again, assuming you have the finances left after running said teenager(s) for the last few years, this should be relatively easy to achieve. Unfortunately it is impossible to fill up a teenager, and even harder to get them to leave their room to scavenge for said snacks. The best you can do is throw chocolate bars at them as they slouch down the hall to head down the park with their mates.

3. That boyfriend/girlfriend they've brought home. The one that is 97% pierced, has decided to stick it to the man by wearing their jacket back to front and rides a motorbike. You've got to try to like them. Because you teenager does. And hey, don't take things on first impressions, your teenager might

simply see something in this person that you don't. They know them better than you. They might be right.[96] Sit down, lob 'em a beer have a chat – this could be the person that co-authors your grandchildren.

4. Enjoy it. You won't get this time again. You know what, this one's true. From birth till they fly the nest. Enjoy the good stuff and survive/learn from the tougher stuff, because down the line you'd sell your own armpit[97] to go back in time and have just one more discussion about not peeing on the floor with your twelve-year old. Each time they get older, that younger version of them no longer exists and you'll miss them. Every single one of them.

5. The best thing you can do with your teenager, assuming they are one of the more common types who grunt, shout or ignore you on a daily basis; whose laundry bill has increased exponentially because of the aforementioned hormones, and whose weekly food allowance seems like it is going to feed a family of 8, is just be there for them. But not too much that they feel smothered. But not so little that they feel abandoned and unloved. You should allow them autonomy and choices,[98] recognise and talk through their big feelings, and always make them feel loved and cared for.

Basically, they're like bigger, smellier versions of toddlers. Just don't tell them I said that. Stroke their pimply brows, whisper to them that of course, OF COURSE they're grown up and important and the world still revolves around them, and teach them how to use the washing machine.

---

[96] They probably aren't.
[97] Even though it's holding your arm on.
[98] But not about actual important things, like whose turn it is to have control over the remote.

Wider Family

If you are lucky, you will have a good support network of family who are always there for you, ready with a gentle word of advice or a good injection of cash whenever you need it. Your parents will be kind, loving and benevolent, and their home will always be open and ready for you to raid the cupboards and lounge about on the comfy sofas.

Your siblings will be smart, funny and successful,[99] and always up for a night out or to listen to you for hours as you whinge on about your latest break up.

Grandparents will be doting on both you and your offspring, and Granny will always slip you a sneaky piece of chocolate like she did when you were a kid,

---

[99] Though not as successful as you, to avoid potential jealousy on your part.

she having neglected to notice that you are already the size of a house based on her habit of feeding you when you were sad, leaving you with a lifelong eating disorder.

Aunt Ethel will consistently tell you that you are her favourite, and graciously point out that in her will that she is leaving everything to you, including Toots the cat who you sincerely hope won't outlive Ethel.

Yeah, right.

The thing with family is, they are all people too. This means they share the same emotional issues with you – in fact they may have kindly shared some of them with you from an early age – and they have their own irritating opinions on how you should be running your life.

If you're very lucky, you won't be able to get away from them, so you may as well accept them. I know, I know – you'd rather poke out your eyeballs with rusty pins, but there really is no other option.

Now, some people[100] say that we 'choose' our family when we are floating around in the primordial soup that is our life when we are not currently inhabiting a body. A lot of people think that is nonsense – if we could choose, why on earth would we not go for the Royal Family[101] or something? Surely you would pick rich, benevolent parents who are able to grant your every financial desire with a flick of their Mastercard? Why on earth would you pick siblings who are just so goddamn annoying?

However, I do think there's something in it. Why would people be so irritating unless you had something to learn from them?

Parents

When you're a child you mostly think your parents exist for two reasons. Firstly to feed you, and secondly to create all sorts of ridiculous rules, solely with the intention of making your life miserable.

'Do not eat that, you don't where it's been.'[102]

'Do eat that, it's good for you.'

'Do not put that in the cat, again.'

'Do take that out of the cat.'

---

[100] Please don't ask us who, we can't remember. Maybe we read it in a Christmas cracker one day or something.

[101] Dear god. Apart from the money I can't imagine anything worse than being related to this bunch of inbreds.

[102] Or, in fact, what it even IS.

'Do not get your head stuck between those railings, again.'

'No you can't walk the 150 mile round trip to Yorkshire to see your mate that moved away.'

'Yes we can walk the 100 yards to school.'

And you are absolutely convinced that none of the other kids at school have to abide by ANY of these rules, simply because there is a boy in your class that is basically bringing himself up because his parents are always at the pub.

There is one other thing that parents are expected to do when we're kids… Know EVERYTHING. Nowadays you can turn any question into an opportunity to practice using some grown-up research techniques,[103] but it wasn't that long ago that parents actually had to have answers. (Notice I said answers; I did not say they had to be correct.) The plethora of entirely made-up information rattling around inside the heads of pre-internet kids is a wonder to behold. It wasn't until I was a least quite a lot of years old that I realised that power stations weren't, in fact, cloud generators, as I had been informed by my hilarious parents. Nowadays parents can know everything, as long as they can distract the kid for long enough to whip out the old pocket internet device and have a quick search.

As we age and reach the wonderful, living, beautiful and not-at-all-nightmarish-for-everyone-involved teenage years, our parents become an irritant we have to live with because we haven't got a job, a form of transportation to go out with out mates or see that boy/girl we fancy – and then a shoulder to cry on when everything goes Pete Tong and it turns out that everything that they had said was RIGHT.

Because, you see, parents were at some time kids too, and although technologies have advanced and social rules have changed,[104] the basics of being a functioning human being, haven't really changed much since the cave person times.[105]

Then we become adults ourselves and the parental relationship, assuming it has survived the previous years relatively intact becomes more like a friendship. Disagreements are still had but now they are in the form of discussion, not argument. Previously they would have been along the lines of,

'Tidy your room!'

'Have you done your homework?'

'No, you aren't wearing THAT skirt outside this house!'

But now they are more:

---

103   Google it.

104   I still can't believe they let the other half of the population vote. Their poor little brains. I do feel for them. They've got enough to worry about carrying those testicles about all day.

105   Except with fewer clubs and more glasses of Chardonnay.

'Oh, you like [insert film name here]?! I found it far too cliched, and I had predicted the finale before the opening credits had finishing rolling.'

Or:

'Really? You think they've done ok? I think the [insert political party here] have pretty much wanked up everything they've done, and mainly to line their own pockets.'

We're all grown ups, we all have opinions but now they are discussed over a cappuccino or a glass of Rosé, and it's nice.

Then, some of us have kids ourselves and it is only then that the true majesty what we owe our parents comes to the fore. It is only when it is you that is having those sleepless nights, days filled with vomit, cleaning up of pooey nappies/bums/backs/headboards, arguments and the continual fear that you are, basically, fucking it all up, that you really realise what your parents gave up for you. It's pretty awesome of them really. Hey, why not go tell them?

Grandparents

These are for 100% fun. They are no holds barred entertainment machines, and for a very good reason. You only exist because they went through the hell of bringing up your parents. You are their reward for this. They have zero responsibility for your upbringing and can therefore be entirely irresponsible when they have you. Sweets, crisps, energy drinks, tree climbing, activities that are both exceedingly fun but also leave your clothes coated in mud all get the thumbs up from these guys because, at the end of the day, they get to hand you back.

Not only are you their reward, you are also their revenge. There's nothing quite like handing back an overtired child filled to the brim with sugar, closing the door and watching from the window, sniggering as the parent tries to wrestle them into the car seat. It's like watching WWF.[106]

Grandparents also have the advantage of knowledge. They did all their living and learning pre-internet. They hold all their information inside their head, not in a black box in their pocket. Birds, trees, animals, choke holds, they KNOW all the cool stuff without having to look it up, and that is actually something rather magical.

Finally, because they bought their house for 89 pence, had all the good pensions and got to retire at an age where their knees still worked, they've got the coolest cars, and nicest houses and biggest gardens and because they've been doing it since

---

[106] Wrestling, not animals. – Actually, either works.

the dawn of time, they're the best cooks. And they understand the fundamental importance of biscuits. Basically, against these guys, your parents didn't stand a chance.

Siblings

These things are great, really truly. And it's interesting how the relationship changes over time; it seems to go in standard steps:

When you're both tiny, you adore each other. You worship them if they are older, and dote on them if they're smaller. You pose together in all sorts of cute moments such as eating mud or pouring cat food down the loo, and make your parents tear up.

As childhood proper hits, you tend to as well. Your sibling is now your own personal punching bag, and any residual affection is replaced by the need to dominate them 100%. This is not play fighting like cute lion cubs; you probably do actually want to kill them. Your parents tear up again – not with joyful pride this time, but with the certainty that they have bred delinquents who will be in Borstal before they're 8, accused of robbing old ladies' pensions.

During teenagerhood, you can practise your total superiority on your sibling, denouncing them as the ugliest/smelliest/least cool being on the entire planet. Ignore them totally, unless they are older and can give you lifts places. Parents have stopped bothering to react to your interactions, and instead act as terrorist negotiators when you are in the same room.

Young adulthood kicks in, and you cautiously look around at your life and realise that your sibling is not that bad, actually. Turns out they are a human being as well. Suspiciously go on nights out with them, marvelling that they seem to be a relatively sorted human being and are, dare we say it, quite nice.

Into later life, you comfortably hit a groove where you find yourself talking to them all the time, valuing their opinion and realising that they might be the only person with whom you can still fall about on the floor with laughter, both of you in stitches remembering the Christmas Aunt Ethel mistook a coaster for Mum's Christmas pudding, or imitating Dad's sneezes. This, my friends, is the heyday of sibling life.

You can use them as your own punching bag when you are both children, then ignore them totally throughout your teenage years because they're clearly not as cool as you and will bring down your street cred, then when you both hit adulthood you will look up one day and discover that actually they are quite nice human beings, that you can share chats and beers and moans about the state of Life with. Plus, you can bitch about the rest of the family in a way that outsiders just won't understand.

Cousins

These guys are generally your first friends as babies, as long as your parents have followed the steps above. You'll be plonked down on a mat together to stare at each other and dribble, while both your sets of parents share their joy at having reproduced. You will be friends with these guys throughout your entire life, even though you will possibly only see each other at family gatherings – you are pretty much given no choice in the matter, being that family will gather, and the grown ups want to do grown up things so 'the kids' are expected to wander off together and do kid things.

They are generally a step removed from Siblings, so hanging out with them will involve a fair bit less physical violence. They are generally cool enough, especially if they are slightly older and have more life experience, that you can hang out with them and your street cred may even be improved.

When you grow up you have the choice whether or not to have anything to do with them – I particularly like the fact that it's like having a ready-made friend who you're also related to, and who can, like your siblings, remember things from your childhood that have other people staring at you blankly.[107]

There is something about people you are related to you – not just that nose that you all inherited from Aunt Ethel's side – that speaks to a primeval part of you. It's like blood senses blood that is similar to its own, like a group of animals who hang out together solely because their stripes are the same colour.

Aunts and Uncles

If you're lucky, your own parents followed the steps above with their own siblings, and they're relatively close and quite like each other, meaning that you may see a fair bit of your aunts and uncles. They are pretty similar to your parents, but enough removed from the authority of actually Being Your Parent that they can spoil you a little more than your own parents – or at least not tell you off quite so

---

[107] My cousins are awesome. Yes, I *am* bragging.

much. If you're even luckier, they will have kids around about your own age, so you can have someone to hang out with at family gatherings (see Cousins).

As well as the aunts and uncles you are actually related to you, there is a 99% chance that you have a whole pile of them to whom you're not actually related. These ones will be your parents' friends, people your parents like enough to pretend to you through your formative years that you are related to, leading to much confusion when you get to an age of actually figuring out family relations, and wondering why Auntie Shirley isn't written on the family tree but Aunt Ethel is, when Auntie Shirley is super cool and lets you experiment with her make up, while Aunt Ethel shouts at you for touching her fancy glass cat ornament and forgets her false teeth when she comes for dinner.

Housing

Have you ever heard the phrase 'An Englishman's[108] home is his castle'? This is a true thing – each and every one of us SHOULD be able to live in our own castle, safe from the marauders and intruders and sabre toothed tigers. And the in-laws.

Life is a trickier thing than that though, isn't it?

Getting hold of your own home, whether you buy it, rent it or build it, is a really difficult thing for many of us, requiring blood, sweat and tears,[109,110] and generally a bucketload of cash.

---

[108] Insert your own gender pronouns here, please. I certainly do. *Dear oh dear, Miss Hancock! 'Englishman' is not a pronoun. I think that it is what in the modern parlance would be called a gendered noun. Nor could you apply the term 'pronoun' to 'his,' which is a possessive pronominal adjective, although it can also be a pronoun (e.g. 'this one is his'), but not here.*

[109] Not guaranteed.

[110] *It is certainly encouraging to see you adopting a Churhillian turn of phrase, young lady.*

The thing is, no one should have to rent. No one should have to hand over half their wages until they die in order to pay for their four walls while substituting luxuries like, oh, food, for example. None of us should have to move back in with our aged parents in order to just save up the deposit. No one should have to give up their precious pets, or decide to rehome their kids, because a rental house does not come with a garden or a built in playpen or enough insurance to cover the damage that these wild creatures may well inflict on a property.

Housing should be available to each and every one of us – it's not like we're asking for a mansion or anything! Just a little place where we can hang our hats[III] and spend our few waking hours after work.

In Ye Olde Days, it was perfectly possible to just build your own house. This is because there were very few of us, and we were all very happy to live without running water or electricity[112] as long as we had a flimsy wall or two to keep out the sabre toothed tigers.

This is no longer possible, due to the aforementioned spread of humanity and the fact that we have basically trawled our planet for all its natural resources already, so there is very little left for the average cave dweller who wants to build their own home. (And if you do decide to go down the cave route, you'd better leave a trail of crumbs, a la Hansel and Gretel, to find your way back through the maze of red tape you will have to navigate.)

You'd think the Powers That Be would be happy to have a wee percentage of us take the pressure off them by providing ourselves with our own living accommodation, wouldn't you? I mean, we can responsibly source our own water and electricity and heating, plus we can create homes that are liveable and we promise not to sue anyone if our roofs fall in. But no. Just no. Living off grid, or living in your very own home that you have built for your very own self, is a great way to find yourself with a snotty eviction notice and even less of a prospect than you had before.

How about living in a van, then? This is even more convenient for our Great Leaders, because we're not even taking up a permanent space. Like a snail, you can move your home about whenever the need grabs you, or when you spot some tasty leaves in the distance. But again, ohhhhh no! You are Not Allowed to do this, and any amount of claiming you are of Romany descent on your granny's side will just not wash.

III   And coats, and shoes, and dog drying towels, and multiple pairs of toddler shoes that they will never wear.

112   You don't miss what's not been invented yet, right?

The thing is, independence is frowned upon. Not paying bucketloads of cash to your government is frowned upon. Stepping out of society enough to be happy is definitely against the rules. Yes, we're pretty grumpy about this too.

You may be moving out on your own for the first time, or settling down with a beloved, or deciding to branch out into the world of Adulthood and paying for the status symbol/security that is your very own home.

Just stroll in, lob a sensible amount of money at someone and all will be well. Maybe some years ago it was. At least the sensible amount of money bit.

But now, it's horrendous. Your outrageous expectation to have a roof over your head and still have enough money to heat it, and maybe eat occasionally, are long gone. We're talking half your salary and if you're unlucky enough to live somewhere expensive, like London, or Somerset, or ALMOST ANYWHERE, you're unlikely to get somewhere that you can fit both ends of your body in at the same time.

You have to have a deposit to buy a house. Houses are expensive so a deposit is a lot of money. Rather hard to save for when you're handing over most of your money to buy someone else's house for them already. And banks won't trust you to lend you the money if you haven't got a deposit. Even though you have spent the last 5 years handing over enough money to buy someone else's house for them. Regularly. Every month. You've BEEN paying off a mortgage.

So. Don't rent because you'll never be able to buy. But don't buy because, well, you'll never be able to buy. This leaves one real option.

Stay with your parents till they die and hope they leave you a house, or enough money to get as deposit for one. Easy.

However you do it, there will be pitfalls and triumphs, successes and failures – and we are here to navigate you through the ins and outs of living in a house. Yes, I know, you've probably been doing this since you were a child – but doing it for your very own self is a whole different thing.

Also, just a disclaimer – we don't know what we're talking about. If you have any pointers for us with regards to how one ends up with a mansion à la Jane Austen, then please feel free to let us know. Email address to follow.[113]

Let's have a wee look at the different methods of living in a house, the ups and downs of each method, and what we can do to make the whole process slightly less hideous for all of us. What I mean is, let's have a good old giggle about how rubbish life can be, and rant together about the unfairness of it all. Yeah!

---

[113] This is a fib. Please don't email us, unless you have a free mansion into which we can move, with sweeping skirts and corsets and things. *More mendacity, Miss Hancock! However, I must agree. I don't want them to email me, either.*

Rent

Renting a house is, generally, how most of us start out.[114] As we are usually quite young when this happens, renting a house is a great way to learn how the rest of life works – you have to hand over most of your monthly earnings, leaving you with a pittance to buy things to keep yourself alive.

Renting can be quite freeing, however – you can move out of the house whenever you want, as long as you give the appropriate notice period and don't write on the walls with your own excrement.

If something goes wrong with your rental, you can usually phone the landlord and get them to come out and fix the boiler/gutters/leaking roof that you have been patching up with gaffer tape and laying out pans to catch the cascading waterfalls, while choking to death on the rapidly encroaching black mould.

That is, if you are lucky enough to get a good landlord. Some of them don't care. In fact, many of them would happily see you patching up the broken gutters with used dental floss, hanging onto the side of the building by a pair of suspenders, rather than coming out to fix any structural damage.

What you want is a landlord who is available, but not TOO available. They should be reachable to come and fix things at the drop of a hat, but not too keen to come and do house inspections every month. (What is the deal with house inspections, by the way? What do they think we're going to do to their beloved bricks and mortar? If they cared about it that much, they should live in it themselves, right?)

Which brings me to the point...

No one, but NO ONE should be allowed to own more than one home. This is a despicable practice, reserved for the rich and arse-holey among us, who have decided that an entire houseworth of wealth and security is not enough, and they must own more, to extort more housesworth of riches from the rest of us that cannot afford to do this.[115] Renting is basically just buying someone else's house for them. Their second home. A spare one. While you can't even have one.

But, we all have to live somewhere. These days, with the rampant spread of humanity, we have to be content with the ruthless cut throat market that is the life of renting a house:

---

[114] Unless you have a trust fund, win the lottery, or get incredibly lucky with a dead relative.

[115] And, to be fair, most of us are just not this arseholey. Or maybe we just can't afford it? Let me know.

- Sometimes you spot the perfect property, go to visit it and discover that the photographs were taken with a fish eye lens, so what looked like a decent sized living room would actually fit comfortably inside the Sylvanian's castle.

- 'Two baths' might make you think that there are two toilets, but actually means that there is one dilapidated shower cubicle about the right size for a hobbit, and a large hole dug in the garden with a loo seat balanced precariously over the top.

- Or, you might go to view a house, declare it to be perfect, sign on the dotted line – then have it whipped out from under you by someone who has offered to pay more than you could ever afford to.

These days, renting is as brutal as a gladiator fight. You may come out of this one alive, but you will probably lose your dignity and quite a lot of your mind.

Or, just for shits and giggles, you can choose to rent a room in a shared house. Read that line again… A Shared House. This means that you move into a house with a bunch of random strangers, and you will be paying them for the privilege of a bed and potentially a shelf in the fridge. It's like a hotel, but without any of the bonuses.

This option is generally reserved for students, or people who are single and free from responsibilities – and it's a great option, really. Unless the people you decide to shack up with turn out to be psychos. Or avid jazz listeners. Or have a penchant for The Lighthouse Family. Or kitchen fascists. You know the type – the ones who can only wash certain pans at midnight, or soak their pulses in pots all over the work surfaces, or regularly take up the kitchen sink to water the house plants. Or help themselves to your special fridge shelf.

Again, we really don't condone murder, buuut if you are renting in a shared house and it all gets too much, we can provide you a watertight alibi. Just saying.

Buy

Owning our own home is the pinnacle of success, right? It's a sign that you have made it through all the other stages – school, college, uni, a good job – and now you are sorted enough to own your own pile of bricks and mortar.

But (here's another one of those!) it's not as easy as all that, is it?

We're surrounded on all sides by judgemental Old People,[116] who bray about how we should be living by ourselves, living within our means, and comfortably affording the mortgage payments.

However, most of our parents' generation bought their houses for £4.50,[117] and managed to own said house within 5 years of buying it, while still having enough money to afford luxuries.[118]

These days, you're considered lucky if you only have to work 70 hours a week and manage to get out of your overdraft for 2 days a month, hanging onto your house by the skin of your teeth and patching up all the broken bits with gaffer tape that you borrowed from the pawn shop.

There are a lot of benefits to owning your own house, don't get me wrong. However, a lot of these benefit are offset by the fact that you are now in charge of your own bricks and mortar. Ergo, you, and you alone will bear the responsibility of fixing it when it breaks.

Yes, you can paint it whatever colour you like, smoke 17,000 fags a day, make a bonfire in the sink because you're grumpy that you don't have a wood burner, and write on the walls with your own excrement. The downside is, now that you own it, you will have to look after it.

No one is going to come and fix that broken roof tile for you – you have to find and pay someone all by yourself. When you've burnt out the bottom of the kitchen sink and got toasted marshmallows stuck in the taps, you are the one who bears the responsibility for finding a plumber. If the boiler goes, the only panicked phone call you are going to be making is to your bank manager, to discuss whether selling your body on the streets is going to bring in enough to get a new one – or indeed warm you up enough to not need one.

Owning your own house as opposed to renting is the equivalent of moving out into your first rental after the Halls at uni. It is just one more step towards gently nudging you to being a completely independent and fully functioning adult.[119] It is bloody terrifying, is what it is!

And there are so many things to consider – what's the area like? Are there regular gunfights or just the occasional stabbing? Is your favourite school in the catchment area or do you have to send your kids off to the local comprehensive, which is tightly bound in barbed wire to stop the students escaping and raiding

---

[116] I hope that's not a dig at me, Miss Hancock! I try very hard not to be judgemental.

[117] £4 10s, although I always work in guineas myself.

[118] Ok, this is not necessarily true. I'm only saying this because I'm bitter about not yet owning my own bricks and mortar.

[119] This is in no way guaranteed.

the local shops? Is it close to work or are you going to have to start sleeping in the office 5 nights a week?

Maintenance

They say that in life only death and taxes are inevitable. This rather fails to take into account homeownership. Sinks WILL leak. Doors WILL stick. Garden gates WILL drop at one end and then not latch properly.[120] Bits WILL just fall off for no obvious reason at 3 a.m. and scare your tits off.[121]

Maintaining your house is a bit like cleaning it. You do it once, and imagine that it is done, DONE for the rest of time! Never again will you have to fix a leaky roof, or re-proof the shed! Erm, sorry, but that, like the cleaning, is not the case.

There is always, ALWAYS Something That Will Need Doing to your house. Whether that is getting around to replacing that broken roof tile that sends a tidal wave into the kitchen when the wind is in the Eeast, or fixing that bit of skirting board that the dog decided was a good substitute for a bone, or replacing the carpet that is so filled with the accumulated filth of the years that you can't remember what colour it once was.

Fixing and replacing stuff on your house is like that bridge that takes so long to paint that by the time they've got to the end, the beginning is all faded and they have to start all over again. Once you've done That Thing that you have been putting off for years, your sneaky house will tap you on the shoulder and point out all the other broken bits that it has been quietly brewing while you were fixing the other thing.

Ah well, though. At least it means you get to wander around B&Q on a Sunday with all the other couples, exchanging world-weary grimaces as you stare at two packets of near identical screws and wonder which one is actually going to fix the Thing and which one will make even more holes and leave you with another Thing that needs fixing.

Renting is a pain, but at least there is the added bonus of having Someone Else whose responsibility it is to stop the whole structure from crumbling into the ground and prevent you from dying of black mould. Owning your own house means that you, and you alone, are responsible. You'll have to get a good book, or carefully cultivate your circle of friends to include plumbers, roofers, decorators, and other such useful bods.

---

[120] I hate gates (not Bill – he seems alright, and rarely drops at one end or refuses to latch properly).
[121] Damn! I miss them.

DIY

DIY is one of those things that you never actually learn, it just finds its way into your psyche by osmosis. One minute you're standing on a little chair at age 5, holding the hammer ready to pass it and feeling like the most important being in the world, the next you're watching yourself in astonishment as you hang shelves and fit skirting boards with a professional little flourish.

When you get your first house, you stand in it, staring around you in disbelief, lost in amazement that there are people in this world who can fit carpets so beautifully, and whose wallpaper doesn't look as though someone released a herd of small burrowing mammals beneath it. By the time you actually own your own home, you are such a pro that you can paper a wall in your sleep, and knock up a little wood storage shed in the half hour between work and bedtime.

Oh, wait… none of this is actually true, is it?

You have a go at wallpapering, because that's what Grown Ups do – and you really need that feature wall. Halfway through you give up, sweating and cursing and realising that you actually should have followed the instructions and that you can't just wing it or make your own wallpaper paste out of PVA and flour and water.

When tiling, you decide that starting in the middle and working your way out is a stupid idea, designed for people who are just not very efficient, and you bang the first one in at the edge of the room, closest to the door. You keep going, congratulating yourself on your clever working – then you get to the edge and realise that they were, in fact, right. Who knew? Out comes the tile cutter, followed by another trip to the hardware store after you have ruined a lot of tiles. Repeat.

Plumbing is one of those important things in life, isn't it? It is important to have ways for water to both enter and leave our homes. So you know that you have a leak, and you have overheard people talking about washers. You know these little things are important, so you arm yourself with a spanner and bury your head under the sink. Ten minutes later you emerge, having narrowly escaped being waterboarded, and shamefacedly call a plumber.

There is nothing like doing DIY and having it actually work. It makes you feel like the most useful human in the world, and you instantly come up with a business plan where you swan about the countryside, breezing into other people's houses and fixing their DIY woes with a click of your fingers. Then, the wonky shelf tips a mug of coffee all over your badly laid carpet and you have to go for a little lie down with the Screwfix catalogue.

There are a great many people whose paid employment is fixing your bodge jobs, or doing the job properly in the first place, so for goodness sake call one of them. Or get a book. Or do an online course. Or, sell your house and buy a new one. Then start the whole cycle all over again. And that, my friends, is your life. For the rest of time.

Décor

One of the great things about owning your own home is that you can make it EXACTLY how you want it. No one is going to tell you that you can't paint all the walls black, or plaster the walls with pictures of Simon Pegg in alluring poses. You can hang up black bin bags to stop the neighbours seeing in, refuse all electric light and choose to live with candles instead. It is YOUR home, YOUR castle, YOUR sanctuary.

The thing is, it turns out that we're all pretty boring at heart.

When you stand in the paint aisle at B&Q, excitedly choosing between Midnight Cloak and Hint Of Bat, you suddenly realise that Aunt Ethel is coming to visit your new abode this weekend. She can't see very well at the best of times, so having your home decorated like a cave will not prevent her from mistaking the bathroom for the kitchen, and weeing on your fancy bar stools.

You imagine welcoming your friends to your new pad, and just know that Gemma, with the long wafty hair, is DEFINITELY going to set it alight on one of the candles.

There's always someone who prefers Nick Frost in alluring poses.

You suddenly realise that you are going to have to decorate your house like a Normal Person, and have a small existential crisis right there in the UK's favourite DIY store.[122] Your hand slides slightly to the right, towards the pastels... You watch it, horrified, but ultimately you are unable to stop it from firmly grabbing the tin of Magnolia. If you're lucky, you can scrabble for a tin of Hot Flamingo on the way to the till, then you can at least have a feature wall.

Maybe a feature wall is just a little tiny part of ourselves that is desperate to come out, that genuinely wants the interior of your house to look like the set of Moulin Rouge. That poor little part; it is reduced to a flame red corner, or a

---

[122] Sorry, Screwfix.

brazen strip of wallpaper emblazoned with twiddly designs and brightly coloured parrots.

Never mind. Maybe you'll have kids one day, and you can live out your desire for brightly coloured walls through them.[123]

Garden

If you are not lucky enough to have a garden then I am truly sorry; this section is not intended as a brag. If you love plants and want to create a greenhouse indoors to pretend that you have green space, then this is, unfortunately your option. Unless you have enough money to buy a ranch with a 4 acre garden,[124] you will have to do what you can with pot plants.

If you don't want a garden – well. Maybe skip this section. We like gardens, and are quite likely to bang on about them a fair bit.

The garden is that bit of your house/flat/bungalow/cave/time travelling phone box that has no walls and a floor made of mud, but is still yours to do with as you wish. It can provide you with yummy, healthy, almost free foods, relaxation, socialising activities and the space for that healthy exercise thing we're all supposed to do.

Gardens are great. You can grow things; host boozy barbecues; practise yoga; sunbathe naked; throw the kids out in it when they're too annoying to have in the house any more, and sneak out for a crafty fag behind the bushes without the Nicotine Police swooping down on you.

Unfortunately, mainly due to the time pressures current lifestyles press on us, the garden often just becomes that annoying square green bit you have to mow once a week. And this is a shame. Here's why:

Veggies

Yummy! Healthy! Virtually free! What a concoction of claims! But, the thing is, they're true! Ok, they're not free in time required to grow them, or in time spent cleaning your nails and washing your clothes afterwards, but still. Not bad!

---

[123] But I bet the fuckers will only rebel by painting everything snowy white. Damn them.

[124] If this is you, then what on earth are you doing reading this book? Get out there and ride off into the sunset, dammit! But not before you buy copies of this book for every single one of your friends and acquaintances, so we can make enough to buy the ranch next door.

Growing vegetables is like having kids, but without the constant screaming, mess, demands for food and having to save them from near destruction several times a day. The first time I ever produced a cauliflower I welled up, imagining that this must be what it feels like to give birth.[125]

(Actually, this is not true at all.)

While vegetables are much easier than exotic flowers, and far more rewarding in terms of stuff you can actually eat, they are almost as useless as toddlers, and their lives are fraught with almost as much danger.

So first you have to work out what you want to plant. **Pro tip:** plant the things you will actually eat. If you are allergic to carrots, don't fill your garden with them.[126] Do you hate green beans? Then just don't grow them.[127]

If you and your family go through 25kg of potatoes each week, why not plant them? If your kids graze on tomatoes like they're sweeties, here's an idea: plant them.[128]

Another great idea is to plant the things that are eye wateringly expensive to buy in the shops. Growing a lovely crop of Artichokes[129] will not only make everyone think you are terribly fancy and clever, but will also save you loads on your cocktail party canape ingredients.

If you have never grown any veggies before, the best way to learn is to just throw yourself right in there. As a general rule, plant some seeds in the spring. Wait for them to pop up. Water them occasionally, and weed them to give them space and prevent fighting over nutrients.[130] Pull, dig or pick them when they look like the sort of thing you might hand over money for in the shops. This method is the easiest and involves the least work and learning, so it has always been my go to.

Another option is to find an Old Man, preferably wearing a flat cap and leaning on a fork, with rows and rows of perfect veggies laid out in front of him. Because he's Old, he's had many, many years of growing veg, and he knows everything there is to know about blight, carrot fly, and how to clean out the armpits from your tomatoes.[131] He has the time to lovingly measure out his compost, make

---

125   Oh, how horrifyingly wrong I was.

126   Unless you live near a riding school and want to donate all your hard work.

127   Especially because, as they are so easy to grow, EVERYONE will be growing them. You won't even be able to give them away, and horses don't eat beans so they are no good to your neighbour.

128   I have no intention of planting my family.

129   The fancy ones, not the gnarled tubery ones that will make you think you have ingested 42 tins of baked beans. Shudder. Not 57 tins?

130   Kudos if you can tell the difference between the weeds and the plants.

131   Yes, this is a thing.

perfectly straight rows to house his little seedlings, and he probably has a billion pots that he will be happy to lend you. The downside about tapping this fine gentleman for his gardening knowledge is that you will never be free of him. He'll pop up over your shoulder when you least expect it, poking your compost disparagingly and frowning at your poorly-thinned onions.

A third option, which may be the best if you want to actually learn how to grow veggies and you don't need flat-capped interlopers criticising your every move, is to get A Book. There are loads of them out there, and they're pretty good at telling you when, where and how to plant pretty much anything. You can, if you are so inclined, stick one of these onto a kindle – but the advantage of a book is that you can take it outside with you and not worry about having to spend thousands to replace it when you drop it into the water butt.

Flowers

These are like the perfect partner. They're pretty, they smell nice and, if you choose the right ones, they die off in the winter and leave you in peace and can be replaced with new, exciting varieties the next spring.

However, these gorgeous blooms can be incredibly picky.[132] You will find that you can create a riot of colour in your garden with absolutely no effort whatsoever, if you are happy to just grow dandelions and daisies.

For the more exotic ones, you will find yourself in a garden centre of a weekend, researching compost, spending your evenings poring through seed catalogues, and voluntarily watching *Gardener's World*.[133]

They are like the worst kind of acting diva; they refuse to turn up unless their every single whim is catered for, and they can pout, sulk and not perform if they find something in their dressing room that is not perfectly to their liking.

They are aloof, demanding and very beautiful – if you can make sure that their every need is taken care of and that they are not expected to actually do anything apart from look gorgeous.

Another downside to flowers and exotic plants scattered through your garden is that some of them are deadly poisonous.[134] You will have to do a bit of homework to make sure that you are not accidentally planting a HEMLOCK when you

---

[132]   Also like the perfect partner.
[133]   No offence Monty. I actually really like gardening shows.
[134]   Also like the perfect partner.

wanted a HOSTA, and for god's sake teach your kids the difference between edible CURRANTS (yum) and HONEYSUCKLE berries (death on a stick).

Wild

This is genius. You get to look cool, friendly to the environment and, currently, right on trend by doing almost nothing. Just let your garden get on with it and when your neighbour is looking nervously at the giraffe leaning over your almost-collapsing fence and scrumping their pears, just state that you're giving the land back to nature. Maximum smug superiority, minimal effort.

In all seriousness, having at least a tiny section of your garden given over to The Wild is actually a really great idea. It's all very well, having a beautifully manicured garden with not one tiny weed daring to show its head, or covering everything with Astroturf,[135] but a bit of natural wildlife needs a place to go too.

You remember bees, right? Those little buzzy guys that pollinate stuff and are literally the main reason humans are alive and able to eat? Yeah, them. They live on nectar, so they need plants that create nectar – luckily for you, these don't have to be crazy exotic ones that needs lots of effort from you. Dandelions are great for bees, and also a great excuse for you to not weed every single patch of your garden. Bees also love lavender, which is another minimal effort plant for you to grow.

As well as bees, there are some other wonderful animals that would love a bit of a wild patch to hide in. Hedgehogs, those spiny little dudes, are increasingly endangered, so leave a little higgledy piggledy patch to possibly entice your very own Mrs Tiggy Winkle. Wild birds are also on the decline, and they love to eat creepy crawlies and slugs and snails,[136] so make sure you have a bit of untrimmed hedge for them to hide in.

Wild bits in your garden are also a great way to teach kids about the great outdoors. Just prepare yourself for the influx of little pots all over the place, containing the dead or dying remains of various small creatures. Teach them about the importance of letting the little creatures go, for god's sake!

---

[135] No, no, **NO!** Just don't do this.
[136] A definite bonus for your veggie patch.

Landscaping

This is just big gardening. With diggers. If your garden is big enough to fit a digger in, congratulations! This is the dream, isn't it? Loads of land, AND Big Boys' Toys[137] to mess about it! What's not to love?

Well, probably the planning, funding, executing, and cleaning tracks of mud from inside your house for the next three years until the project is completed. Basically, everything apart from the finished result.

But oh, that finished result! It will be so worth it. Gorgeous ponds cascading down into a plunge pool; staggered raised beds made with railway sleepers; trailing drooping elegant foliage and carefully placed trees... Mmmm. Excuse us while we pop off for a little lie down.

Actually, you don't necessarily need a massive garden in order to do landscaping. Landscaping is just a fancy word for Making The Most Of The Space. Any sized garden can be landscaped and made to look pretty darn fancy. Having different heights seems to be the way forward; so you can always just balance a few pots on top of some old pallets. Maybe make an unseen drop down to another level of the garden so that an unwary guest ends up face down in the pond? Might not be actual landscaping, that, but it would be a bit of a chuckle, wouldn't it?

There are a great many books and online resources to help you on your landscape garden, that some rude people among us describe as being as good as porn. We, obviously, being so innocent and all, would not be able to comment on such things.

Basically, we know very little about landscaping,[138] so feel free to send us your pictures, ideas and finished results so we can tell you more about it in the next book.

---

137 We don't actually believe that heavy machinery is only suitable for boys. We're not the Yorkie ad.
138 Can you tell?

Pets

This is as tough section for me. When I was a young'n our family home was rammed with creatures. Cats, dogs, rabbits, mice, chickens, ducks, my sister, guinea pigs and, almost certainly, fleas. And it was great. Ok, it was sometimes little bit hairy, or feathery, or downright animally, but it was generally great.

But now, I have a daughter who is allergic to virtually everything. Our home is animal free, and It feels bad for the soul. I admit, the lack of cleaning up is lovely, and means we have more time for other family things – but the look on my kid's face when meeting other people's pets is both wonderful and saddening at the same time.

There is possible light at the end of the tunnel though. Recently we did some rat sitting for a nephew's rat, Gerald (the rat, not the nephew). The allergic kid touched it... and didn't explode. She might be rat-proof. We have found a pet we can have.

If you're anything like the majority of humanity, you prefer the company of most animals to most people. This is, let's face it, because the majority of animals are nicer than the majority of people.[139]

Pets of this world vary from the standard cats and dogs, to the more exotic, such as monkeys, tigers and crocodiles. If you've ever tried to house-train a crocodile, you may be aware that you might well be better off with a fluffy kitten – these guys still have teeth, it's true, but they're much less likely to kill you.

It starts with childhood, doesn't it? I bet you were also once campaigning for your very own dog/cat/tortoise, to the irritation of your parents – 'I'll walk it and feed it and clean it out and everything!' you wail, being totally sure that this is what would happen, despite your parents' sure and certain knowledge that this enthusiasm would last about a week and a half, after which they themselves would be landed with the full responsibility of that dog/cat/tortoise, despite the fact that they didn't want it in the first place.

They know this, because this pet obsession is something that they themselves once experienced. This is a time-honoured tradition that is passed down through the generations, and has been a tradition since the days when the first cave child brought a baby sabre toothed tiger home on a lead made from a vine and 'Ug'd!' at its parents in a pleading fashion.

If you were lucky, you had a tolerant, long-suffering parent who was willing to foster your love of all things fluffy, and you would have had a long succession[140] of hamsters, gerbils, rabbits, guinea pigs, and maybe even a cat or a dog.

My own long-suffering parent took it one step further; once my brother and I spotted an ad for a 'Fruit Bat' in the local paper. We begged and begged, planning elaborate bat cages and picturing ourselves riding down the road on our bikes, with a well trained bat who had been taught to fly to the fist. Mother relented, and called the number – only to find that 'Fruit Bat' was a dog. We lost interest after that. After all, there is no dog in the world that can be taught to fly to the fist.

Once you have grown up and left home, you can make your own decisions about pets. You may think that you would instantly fill your home with cats,[141] dogs and llamas – but the thing is, you start to realise that your parents were right. Who is going to feed it, walk it, and clean it out? That would be you. You

---

[139] Though I wouldn't necessarily say this about venomous spiders.

[140] I use the words 'long succession' because these guys just die for a pastime. Not really the best pets for kids, are they – unless you want to teach them about mortality early, and see them trembling under their bedclothes every time the Hoover comes out, remembering the demise of poor Fluffy.

[141] This is the dream...

suddenly realise that actually, there is very little time or money, and you content yourself with a houseplant instead. You eventually kill it through neglect, and realise that you probably aren't much cut out for pet ownership anyway.

Pets are actually pretty darn wonderful. Having a cat can reduce your blood pressure;[142] dogs can fill your life with exuberance and joy and can make you get off the sofa at least once every day (though you won't thank them for this when it's cold and raining – sadly, dogs still need to move their bowels in the winter); snakes can make you look cool and brooding, and having a pet spider will make everyone think you're incredibly brave and 'ard.[143]

The one piece of advice I can give about getting a pet is: do your homework. If you live in a tiny flat, it's best not to get a St Bernard. For those who live in log cabins by a vast forest, a handbag dog may not be your best bet, unless you're a fan of your beloved pet being eaten by wildlife. Is anyone in your house allergic to pet hair? There are plenty that come naked, so maybe some sort of furless variety is what you need.[144] Keeping a cockerel in a shared house will probably be frowned upon. And, most importantly, despite the rumours, you can't keep a penguin in the bath.

Some pets are dicks though, don't get me wrong. There's the aforementioned curtain acrobatics, yes – but we haven't yet talked about toilet habits and table manners. And, there's a lot of chewing. This is fine, after all you've bought them special toys, at great expense, to help their teeth and give them something fun to do. But, when the object of choice is every single one of your left shoes, it becomes less of an endearing habit.

There are soooo many pets that you can choose from, but to keep things simple, we're just going to have a look into a few of the most common:

Dog

Dogs are just the best, aren't they? They arrive wrapped up in the cutest exterior you ever saw, and steal your heart within seconds. You can laugh at their funny antics, amaze yourself with how much they already seem to love you, and melt with adoration when they fall asleep in a furry pile mid play, the equivalent of a toddler falling asleep in their dinner. It's a good job they're this cute, because

---

[142] Except when they use your expensive Laura Ashley curtains as a climbing frame.

[143] Though you'll probably find they won't improve your dating record.

[144] Unless you don't like the one who is allergic, and want to encourage them to move out or drown in their own secretions.

then you don't mind QUITE so much the amount of pee and poo you will spend the next few months sponging out of your soft furnishings. Then they grow up and chill out (unless you were crazy and got a Spaniel), and they're still just as wonderful – though now they can usually find their way to the garden to pee and poo. They do smell a lot worse when they're older though.

Cat

Cats were worshipped as gods during Egyptian times, and they clearly have not forgotten this. As any cat person will tell you, one does not own a cat... The cat owns you. Like most babies, they start out small and cute and loveable, despite the fact that friends will become alarmed that you have started self-harming, as you suddenly resort to long sleeves in summer to hide the bloody mess your arms have become since little Duchess arrived in your life. Pretty soon, you will be jumping like a waiter to the sound of a paw snap, ready and willing to do your furry overlord's every bidding, in the desperate hope that they will reward you with a crumb of affection. Most of the time, they'll fix you with a baleful glare and turn their back on you. You have been warned.

Rabbit

Rabbits have it all, don't they? They're cute, fluffy, great at using up those out-of-date veggies, and they take very little maintenance. You can even house train a rabbit and keep it in your house, safe in the knowledge that they won't slobber all over your houseguests, or wake you up at 4am by sitting on your face as a way to demand food. They're also pretty clever, and you can have hours of fun constructing them little obstacle courses and teaching them to jump over miniature fences. However, they can also be pretty 'orrible, especially the girl ones,[145] and they have a terrifying preference for eating electrical cables.

Hamster

These are the most usual choice for doting parents wishing to give their beloved child a sweet pet to ease them into the world of responsibility. However, they're not the most suitable pets for children, are they? They're generally terrified of

---

145 Quite similar to the human types.

interaction and will scoot around their cage as you try to get hold of them, then will sink their little teeth into your finger if you do manage to grab them. They are nocturnal, so will be boringly asleep during the day, then manically wild through the night. Many a household lies awake in the wee hours, gritting their teeth, listening to the relentless pounding of the wheel and seriously considering getting the Hoover out.

Gerbil

Tiny, rat-like creatures. They are actually seriously cool; they come from Foreign Parts and can burrow and munch and crawl about with the best of them. They look adorably cute when they munch on a nut. They are less likely to suck on your blood than a hamster. They might not eat their babies when they inevitably breed.

However, a gerbil is just as likely to peg it for no reason whatsoever, leaving your beloved infant traumatised in the morning when they lift their pet out for a cuddle to find that it has gone the same way as the goldfish.[146]

Guinea Pig

Finally, the perfect pet for children and adults alike! This thing is cute, fluffy, likes a cuddle, and is fairly low maintenance. You can keep them indoors or out (though as wild creatures they are definitely better off outside) and they are daytime venturers so won't keep you awake throughout the night with their antics. They will happily munch on your vegetable leftovers, and, while they can't be house trained, their droppings are so innocent and inoffensive that you can happily pick them up and pretend they're raisins.[147]

However...

Guinea pigs, when scared (or excited, or a little bit nervous, or just for the hell of it) make a noise that will have your neighbours calling the police, terrified that a hideous bloody murder is taking place next door. Honestly, the noise that comes of of these tiny little bodies is just so ridiculously disproportionate. 2/10.

---

[146] Though it is not recommended that you flush a gerbil down the loo. This is a recipe for a rather large plumber's bill

[147] Don't do this.

Rat

Despite their reputations, rats are actually seriously cool. They are intelligent, loving (yes, really), great fun to have around and are less likely to peg it for no reason than some of the other rodent types. They do pee constantly, however,[148] and if you have a boy one you will be disconcerted by the sight of him dragging his enormous testicles all over your soft furnishings. Allergic children are less likely to explode when handling these guys, making them a great choice.

Snake

If you are looking for a soft, cuddly pet, who welcomes you coming home and gives you cuddles and affection to remove the stresses of your day, don't get a snake. Yes, we can keep snakes as pets, and yes, as long as you have a good sized vivarium and have researched the best ways to feed and keep them happy, then they'll be pretty good. But, keeping a snake always comes with a degree of barely repressed terror.

These guys, some breeds of them, are capable of killing a grown man in less than 2 minutes. They're fascinating, fun, interesting and a good novel and exciting pet. But, they are actually terrifying.

Apparently, two of humanity's most feared creatures are snakes and spiders. This is an instinctual fear, based on our early cave person days, when most wriggly things or crawly things could kill us with a single glance. These days, it is still totally understandable to be scared of snakes. If anyone gives you gyp about it, just tell them that you are channelling your inner cave person, and that if they had any instincts they would be running for the hills too. They should shut up after that.

Spider

See 'Snake' above.

---

[148]   They're a lot like Aunt Ethel in this regard.

Fish

These are the ideal pets.[149] They look beautiful, require very little maintenance, and they don't really have personalities, so it's not the end of the world when one of them dies. You just get another one – they pretty much look identical anyway.

Just try to avoid them dying in traumatic circumstances, like letting the cat play in the tank; replacing the tank water with water from the kettle, or accidentally swapping the fish food for salt. This method means you can enjoy your fish friends for many years to come.

Birds

I really don't like seeing small birds in cages – they're meant to be soaring wild and free – but I had to include a bird section because… Chickens. These guys are just fantastic. Unlike most other pets they will pay their way, providing you and your family with daily delicious eggs, making all those other freeloaders look like lazy teenagers. Plus, they are just hilariously funny. They can't fly but they think they can, so they flap about like, well, headless chickens. And have you ever seen a chicken jump? They do it like Irish dancers, with wings tucked tightly in and fluffy bloomers on display. They are descended from dinosaurs, which is absolutely hilarious – until you try to imagine a 30 foot long chicken. Admit it, that is pretty terrifying.[150]

You will almost certainly find, when you get your pet, that they will become more special to you even than your own offspring. Pets are just so awesome! They're pretty much always happy; they are good for your physical and mental health, and they very rarely get grumpy about you always having control of the remote control.

---

[149] Unless you get the Really Fancy Types.
[150] I think this is the case with most pets and family members.

Cars

When you think about it, cars are actually a bit scary. Have you ever looked up the facts and figures for how many people die on the roads every year? Don't. Just don't do it.

However, we do need these piles of potential death to get us out and about – especially as we no longer live in tribal society where you can easily pop in on Aunt Ethel because she literally lives next door. Some people are happy about this change in our society, and remember that it is totally fine to bail on the in-laws because the car has broken down,[151] but in order to get to work or visit people you actually like, you probably need some wheels.

But, these wheels do come with a lot of their own problems, especially in today's modern world. Gone are the days when you could just hit it with a spanner, or tie up the broken bits with baler twine and hope for the best. These days we have onboard computer systems; automated thises and thats, and even cruise control for those who are brave enough. And don't even get me started on electric cars.[152]

---

[151] Again. Just remember to keep track of how often you use this excuse, or they might take pity and buy you a new car, so that you can visit them. All. The. Time.

[152] I mean this. I don't know anything about them, so I will probably just make up a load of nonsense so that you think I know what I'm talking about.

Driving

As soon as you have passed your driving test, you are free to be released onto the roads. How terrifying is this?! A whole horde of teenagers, who still have to be bribed to clean their bedrooms, being allowed to be let loose on the roads, in control of machines that can wipe out lives in seconds! **Arrrrgghhhhh!!**

It's easy to forget that we were once a part of this horrifying horde. Once upon a time, we too were young, carefree and reckless, and enthusiastic about gaining some treasured freedom and not having to deal with the cringeworthy shame of being driven around in your dad's rusted old Volvo whose exhaust pipe falls off for a pastime.[153]

You casually get in behind the wheel of your first Escort that all your family clubbed together to buy you, hiding your trembling hands and hoping that the sweat dripping off your palms will not prevent you from gripping the steering wheel. You nervously kangaroo hop down the road, ignoring the tears of pride in your parent's eyes as well as the screams of laughter from the local Yoof. You pull up outside your mate's place, filled with the joy and slight feelings of superiority that come with knowing that you passed your test first. And then…?

You become the taxi driver; the late night McDonald's bringer; the Sober One on nights out; the one who pays for all the fuel and turns a blind eye when one of your 'mates' throws up out the window and splatters the car behind with barely digested Bacardi Breezers.

Then, after a few years on the road and probably several new/old cars as each one eventually dissolves into rust because you're young and you can barely afford the fuel to get you about, let alone buying a New Car that might last longer than 6 months, you join the ranks of the tired, the cynical, the heavy-footed speeders who cruise at 45 through a 30 zone because you know the speed camera is broken.

Congratulations! You have joined the special group of people who are allowed to huff and tut at learner drivers and bend or break the Highway Code on a daily basis. You know for a fact that your driver's license is out of date but you get by on hoping that you never get stopped or have an accident.[154] You drive your car despite knowing that it probably needs something quite major fixed, and you deal with it by sticking your fingers in your ears and going 'La la la!'[155] to drown out

---

[153] Generally in front of a group of very attractive members of the opposite sex.

[154] Actually this is a daily thought for me on every single car journey I make. It's a good survival strategy, I feel. If you are from the DVLA, this never happened. Honest.

[155] This is not recommended. Keep your hands on the steering wheel and buy some headphones.

the scary knocking noises. You desperately hope that you never have to sit another driving test, because you know for a fact that you'd fail on just about everything.

Maintenance

Maintaining your car is not as much hard work as maintaining your relationship[156] – unless you're one of those petrol heads who spends a lot of time loving and polishing your car, and doing unspeakable things to the exhaust pipe.

For most of us, maintenance involves making sure there is screen wash and oil, and sending the beast for its yearly MOT.[157] Maintaining a car in good working order should not be more hassle than this.

But, services! This involves handing over extortionate amounts of money to your mechanic, who will suck his teeth ominously, change a filter or two, then tell you that it will cost you much more than that original, extortionate amount because his back is particularly bad that day and it took him a lot longer than he thought it would, plus the moon is in Scorpio and this will affect his credit rating. Or some such nonsense.

Then there are the tyres! Your car won't run around without these things being in good nick, so woe betide you if you drive over a thistle or a nail or bump gently into a kerb! Cars are a bit like footballers (see Sports) in that they just can't cope with an issue that you would just grimace and get on with. That being said, they provide you the means to get about the countryside, so we'll forgive them their many misdemeanours.

Fixing

I like to think I'm a modern kind of gal. I know what a dipstick is, and I even know how to stare knowledgeably at the level on the stick, wondering frantically if there's enough oil to get me to the garage or if I'll blow up on the way, or even if the *car* will..

I can change a tyre – in fact, I once did so on the way back from a christening, teetering in my high heels in my fancy dress[158] – but this is about my limit.

---

156 Mainly because you can pay someone else to do it.
157 Clutching your hair and nibbling your nails because you know there is a horrible knocking noise that you have been dealing with by turning the music up louder.
158 This is actually a big fat lie. I got as far as jacking the thing up and getting the spare tyre out, then a big burly man pulled over and offered to help. I have to admit, I fluttered my eyelids demurely and let him. In my defence, it was a really nice dress and I didn't want to get it dirty.

I admit to not being a mechanic (if I was, I might be richer than I am) but I am willing to learn! These days, my 'fixing' of cars is limited to:

- Adding windscreen washer fluid and feeling like I've fixed the world's problems

- Turning up the radio louder to drown out the knocking noises

- Lifting the bonnet and staring knowingly at the engine

- Giving the car a stern talking to

- Smacking the dashboard in the hope of frightening it into behaving

- Feeling guilty and offering it pats, cuddles and a refill of fuel if it makes it home

There are a great number of books out there that can help you to deal with your car's temperamental issues – and, of course, you can find any amount of information on the internet. Sometimes this can be quite amusing too; you type in your particular question and may come up with a forum of questions and answers. Some of these people will make you feel like you actually have a clue – at least you know one end of the dipstick from the other.

The thing is, if you're not a mechanic, you shouldn't actually be trying to fix anything to do with your car. I once got so mad I whipped out a starter motor, whacked it in a vice and started hitting it with a hammer to make it do the thing it was meant to do (i.e. start the engine). I eventually threw my toys out of my pram, advertised my beloved camper van as 'Spares or Repair'.[159] A bloke arrived, put the starter motor in the other way around, then started up and drove away my beloved Tinkerbell.

You may think you know Stuff, but actually you don't. You need a trained professional. Seriously, just take it to the garage. Don't be a hero. And, also, protect the rest of the innocent road users. I don't want to be faced on my drive with your dodgy car that you have tried to fix yourself and therefore made more dodgy.

---

[159] The biggest insult that can be levelled at any car, ever. I'm so sorry, Tinks.

Health

This is something I highly recommend you have. Having no broken bits, lungs with the capacity of an oil tanker and the best heart the doctor has ever tested[160] makes life far easier to skip through. In fact, it makes skipping easier too. When young this is relatively easy. You wake up and everything works. Even into teenager years, when you live off of pie and cheap spirits, you can still bounce out of bed, entirely unaffected by the pubful of booze you inhaled the previous night.

Unfortunately, age happens and as age goes up, so do health issues. Some of these are pretty much generic. Bad knees, stiff back and hangovers that make you want to remove your own head happen to most of us. But on top of that you get your own personal turmoils. Hands that hurt if the wind changes, ears that

---

160　I actually got told this by my doctor. I almost dropped my fag into my bottle of vodka.

ring on Thursdays, one leg getting slightly shorter than the other, developing an allergy to wheat, milk, animals, the Mrs, temperature.[161]

Basically you have two options. As you get older spend more and more time maintaining your health. Eat nothing fun, run round in circles for no reason. Don't have any fun.[162] Or, laugh about your ridiculous ailments over a glass of wine. Strangely this last one has perennially proven to be more popular.

Health is another thing that, if you are lucky, you have taken for granted for the majority of your youth. You will have caught colds, tummy bugs, maybe the odd bout of flu, possibly broken a bone or two – but you won't have suffered any life changing or chronic health issues. Or, maybe, you DID have a chronic health condition but managed to chuckle your way through it, knowing that your youth and beauty would see you through.

Health is one of those things that your parents would worry about; holding you back from essential play time by insisting you wear warm clothes, get enough rest, and, god forbid, eating healthy meals. You knew, for a sure and certain fact, that you were totally immortal and that playing outside in your underwear in a blizzard would have no detrimental effect on your health, in the same way that living on chocolate and crisps would simply furnish your body with the correct quantities of nutrients and minerals to see you grow up big and strong.

As you get older though, this all starts to change. You slowly start to become increasingly aware of your own mortality – this incrementally increases until the age of about 35, when you suddenly realise that your every waking thought concerns one of the many hideous ways you will, inevitably, die.[163]

There are a billion and one things in this world that will kill us, and your own body, annoyingly, turns out to be one of these things. This vessel, that you thought was on your side and was as concerned as you yourself are with keeping you alive, suddenly turns on you, like a snake in the grass. You have been looking after it for years,[164] loving it, and totally relying on it to get you through the trials and tribulations of life, when suddenly it starts acting up.

You'll know when the dreaded Age Catches Up With You, and there are a few tell tale signs that you can be sure are only there because you are getting old. Have a browse through this little tick list:

---

[161] This is actually A Thing. It's called Cold Urticaria. On a cold windy day you end up with skin like Freddie Kruger.

[162] There is one exception to this rule. But you generally need someone else to join in, and if you are doing the rest of this health maintenance stuff it is likely that they won't want to.

[163] Or is this just me? I am a bit mental. Buy this book, then I can afford more therapy.

[164] Come on, we all know this isn't true.

- You can't get off the sofa without making that *'Oooooofff!'* noise.

- You start to notice aches and pains in places that you didn't know COULD have aches and pains.

- It's harder to recover from nights out, exercise, slipping down the steps, or having one or two nights where you dare to go to bed after 10pm.

- Your GP rolls his/her eyes and hides when he/she sees you coming.

- You Google each and every new symptom, diagnosing yourself with a terminal disease nearly every time.

All of a sudden, you have to start looking after yourself. Pah, gah, urgh, and other such noises! Do I HAVE to? Can't I just keep going, running on caffeine and no sleep and the occasional night of binge-eating kebabs? Surely, my loyal body will just continue, despite all of this abuse?

After you've spent a few half decades taking your body for granted, completely neglecting it and treating it like an abused partner, it might actually start to protest at being treated so badly. Maybe it's time to give your bod a bit of a break? It can be quite easy, and even (shocked gasp) quite pleasant to look after yourself.

- **Drinking water** is one of those essential things that helps to keep you alive. Adding just an extra pint or two into your daily regime will not only help to keep you alive longer, but it can also be really good for your skin. Not, obviously, as noticeable as a chemical peel, say, but it can help.

- **Sleep,** unless you're secretly a cat, is pretty much just the thing that gets in the way of your fun. But, unless you're Margaret Thatcher,[165] you are going to need more than 2 hours a night. It makes you less grumpy, it improves your metabolism, it helps you stay alive. Result!

- **Exercise** is a word that generally makes me shudder. However, you can do it without setting foot inside a gym, thus tricking yourself into thinking that you're not exercising at all. Go for a walk on a beach (nice), wander through a forest (also nice), go for a jog with a friend (maybe not quite so nice, but you can reward yourselves with coffee and cake afterwards). They say 'Use it or lose it' and this can be applied to bodies, and muscles and joints that actually do what they are meant to do.

---

[165] And if you are, please put this book down and pop off to kill yourself so you're a little bit more dead.

- **Eating** is another one of those things that is absolutely essential in the old Staying Alive game. However, some foods will help you stay alive better than others. Now, I am aware that this opinion will not make me very popular, but McDonald's meals don't actually count as food. In the immortal words of Croc Dundee: 'Ya can live on it... But it tastes like shit.' Throw in a night of extra vegetables, ditch the 14th biscuit, work out how to cook that ready meal yourself from fresh ingredients. It'll do you good, plus it works wonders in the Impressing The Opposite Sex malarkey.

Obviously, we're not suggesting that you start panicking about your health and spending half your days Googling the Age-Defying Fancy Diet That Will Keep You Alive Forever, or spending vast amounts of money on a Chinese/Tibetan/Indian guru who hails from Croydon and changed their name to Chi.

But, keeping half an eye on your bod is a good idea.[166] Maybe have a few nights every week where you don't drink the entire bottle of wine and fall asleep on the sofa? Possibly skip that takeaway that you don't really need (yes, I know it's yummy and convenient, but what about those veggies that you bought and promised to use, that are mouldering in the fridge? Save them, give them purpose!) A bit of exercise probably won't kill you,[167] and it can be quite fun – plus there's the added bonus of it potentially keeping you alive for longer.

---

[166] As long as I can use the other half to keep an eye on other people's

[167] Unless you were the guy that invented jogging. Not a very good advert, was it?

Appearance

You can try as hard as you like to pretend that you are all Zen-like and Buddhist-y about how you look, but let's face it – even the most confident among us would like to think that we are not hideous enough to make small children howl and flee, and set off the local dog population every time we dare show our faces outside of their customary paper bags.

Some people spend A LOT of time on their appearance. I mean A LOT. And a lot of money too and I used to think those people were silly. Its what's on the inside that counts! Do they not realise that? But as I have aged I have realised that this was unfair of me. If that's what floats your boat; if that's what makes you feel good; if that's what you need to face the world – then go for it.

Our appearance is what people see BEFORE what's on the inside, and what we make our first judgements on. Hipster beard, 2 foot bell bottoms, jumper round your shoulders – we all take these things as signalling a certain type of person. Our appearance is in many ways a mirror of what's inside.[168]

...But then, a lot of this judgement is based on people's pre judgements of what a person's appearance means that they might be. For example, my dad used to make me cross the road, holding tightly to my hand, every time someone with tattoos was coming the other way. Now I am a Grown Up, many of my most beautiful and gentle friends are inked from head to toe, and guess what? It doesn't change the fact that they are beautiful souls. It just makes them look cooler than the rest of us.

I used to think spending loads of time and effort and money on appearance was just plain old narcissism and deliberately took the opposite route, but I have recently realised that going round looking like[169] a used tea bag that had had a really bad day may have held me back in life[170] and I was a muppet for judging people for spending time on it. Sorry, you lot.

Ageing

For most people, maintaining a less than hideous exterior takes a lot more effort in later life than it did when you were twenty. In Them Days, you could down a rugby player's worth of booze on a Friday, indulge in a takeaway worthy of Smithy on Saturday, then lounge around all day in your pyjamas on Sunday, never once taking even a sniff of the outside world except when you needed to stagger down to the corner shop for more milk and beer. And, you would still leap out of bed fresh faced as a daisy, on Monday morning, cheerfully pissing off your older colleagues by announcing how much you drank and how little you did, making them feel even older by comparison.

Those days are long gone, my friend.

It turns out that if you abuse your body and take it for granted, it will reward you by not being its Best Self. Understandable, really. I mean, if you had filled me with unexpected amounts of alcohol and then made me do a pole dancing class, I may be slightly grumpy with you. The difference between me and your body is that I can articulate my anger about being forced into exercise by using words, whereas the only way your body can express its displeasure is by causing

---

[168] OK. Ignore the 90s. Jeans and a t-shirt wasn't really a mirror of anything.

[169] And smelling, like and having the charisma of...

[170] THAT explains my failure with the opposite sex. I'm definite that this time what's inside wasn't AT ALL relevant.

you pain, providing you with teenager-worthy spots, and protecting itself from your abuse with an insulating layer of fat.

You may remember being young and careless; trying on different skirts with your bestie and assuring each other repeatedly that you are each the most beautiful creature the other has ever seen.[171] You know you look good, despite the usual teenage anxieties. You parade around the town and the clubs, relishing in your Youth and dewy skin. You ignore all the things the your mum tells you about getting early nights, drinking enough water and using moisturiser. After all, it clearly hasn't worked on her, has it?

Then you hit 25.[172] It starts with one little stray grey hair. You laugh gaily, and tear it out by its tenacious roots, certain that you will not see another until you are ACTUALLY old. But, that little stray has told all its mates, and they will soon be there in a triumphant, gleeful swarm, covering your whole head before you can say, 'Roots and highlights please'.

You may think this is bad! But, with the grey hairs comes the (collective gasp of horror) The Wrinkles.[173] It's all very well to tell yourself that they are a sign of the beautiful life you are living – after all, if you never smiled, you'd never have crow's feet,[174] but no one is ecstatic that their face is starting to resemble a less than attractive scrotum. We're not saying that any of THEM are attractive, but they're better as they are then sitting on your face.

Then, if grey hairs and wrinkles weren't enough, some sort of signal is sent to your body, sometime after the age of about 30. that tells it that it no longer needs to metabolise food quite so well. You may notice a little extra chub after one particularly indulgent Christmas, that in previous years you managed to shed almost as quickly as the New Years Eve hangover. Then… Suddenly, you can't.

Age creeps up on you, like a Peeping Tom shuffling along behind the bushes – you notice it, and it's a little bit irritating, but not quite enough to sound the alarm or ready the pepper spray. Then, before you know it, you can't fit into your jeans any more and you are berating shop staff for putting the wrong size out on the hangers. It clearly states that it's your size, so how come you can barely drag it up over the top of your knees? Obviously, dodgy labelling. Clearly. Yes, that's what it is.

---

[171] Whilst, obviously, being crippled with inner self doubt and body dysmorphia.

[172] -ish. It may come sooner or later for you, but believe us, it will come.

[173] I'm sorry, Miss Hancock; I couldn't stop myself using a wrinkly typeface.

[174] Unless you are chronically short sighted and squint a lot. Combine this with smiling a lot, and you'll look 70 by the time you're 35. Trust me. I know.

You may be one of the lucky ones, who has been blessed with good genes and will look about 25 for the entirety of their lives. You may be able to eat a roast dinner and sink 7 pints of stout every day, get by on 2 hours of sleep and get your only fluid intake from multiple cups of strong, black coffee.

For the rest of us, there comes a time when we actually have to Make An Effort. This may simply involve getting a few more hours of sleep or drinking a bit more water, or you might decide to include vegetables other than the potato in your diet.

Hair

Body Hair

I have a beautiful friend who has got past the Leg Hair Shaving nightmare, by giving up shaving them entirely. She calls it the Arsehole Filter – anyone who is offended by the fact that women have body hair[175] is clearly not someone who deserves her time, attention or even a first thought. I applaud this hugely. Why should we not triumphantly parade our bodies, happy in the skin and fur with which we have been provided?[176] Since when was it acceptable to decide that the most sexually attractive bodies are the ones which look most like children?[177]

Don't get me wrong; I am a firm advocate that one of the nicest feelings in the world is climbing into clean bedsheets, with newly shaven legs. Generally, my excess hair snags on the duvet cover and causes duvet distribution issues – but for those short, sweet few days of a year where my legs do not remind me of our chimp ancestors,[178] I do enjoy the feelings.

Of course, this in itself comes with guilt. I think of my beautiful friend, so true to herself and strong in her ideals – and I hang my head while I reach for the razor, weeping tears of betrayal for the sisterhood with every single smooth stripe I uncover from its customary fuzz.

---

[175] But but but! We've all seen those razor adverts, where a gleaming model runs a shaving device up and down her legs when there is clearly nothing to shave off! Aren't women all like this? Gasp! How horrendous! Anyone would that think that we are mammals, albeit useless ones whose body hair would not sustain us for more than one night in a mild English summer.

[176] I can think of a few good reasons once someone reaches my age and decrepitude, Miss Hancock.

[177] Before you depilate yourself to within an inch of your life, (I never do) ask yourself for whom you are doing this. If it is a bloke, ask him why he is offended by a normal, natural woman who grows hair in places. Then suggest he waxes HIS crotch. Then watch him run.

[178] I shall not launch into a long discussion of the origins of the human race, Miss Hancock. Suffice it to say that we are NOT descended from chimpanzees.

Face Hair

If you are a bloke, you will have experienced Face Hair for a very long time. You may love it or hate it, and you may sometimes flip between these two feelings, possibly linked to how lazy you are feeling and how recently you bought new razors. But, as a girl, Face Hair is not something that we are used to, nor do we expect it.

Apart from eyebrow maintenance and the odd moustache wax, we can pretty much be confident in the fact that we will never grow a beard worthy of competing in one of those strange competitions.

Oh ho ho, chuckles Life. That's where you're wrong

Age brings us all sorts of joys – giving less of a shit about what people think, and starting to realise that life is actually pretty damn good – but it also brings woes. Facial hair is one of those things. Why, oh WHY do I need a little horde of chin hairs? What evolutionary purpose do they serve? Is it simply to protect me against unwanted pregnancy by making me totally repellent to the opposite sex?

And, the worst thing about them is, they hide. You may have closely inspected the lower half of your face before you left the house, fairly confident that your head hair has not slipped today. Then, you catch sight of yourself in someone else's mirror, in different light, and there it is, waving gleefully at you as it wends its sneaky way across your face. And obviously you don't have any tweezers with you, so you grasp it with your fingers and try to yank it out by its tenacious roots, only to give up half an hour later and resign yourself to going to live in a jungle. Maybe Tarzan will find you attractive.

Head hair

It's our crowning glory, isn't it, that thatch that sits on top of your bonce? Hair is something the defines us; contributes to our identity; helps us feel able to step out into the world like a L'Oreal ad, swishing our locks and prancing about like we hadn't a care in the world.

On a good day, that is. On a bad day, your hair can make you feel like you belong under a rock with the other worms. You may feel so self conscious that you resort to a hat, a paper bag, or hacking it all off with a pair of child's scissors.[179] It feels as though your scalp is prickling under the horrified glances of the rest of the world, and you can't wait for the day to be over so you can go home, smash all your mirrors and invest in a wig.

---

179   We wouldn't recommend this, surprisingly.

It's hard when your entire day's happiness is based on what the excreted keratin growing from your scalp looks like, isn't it? But hey, that's life.

Your hair will probably go through a number of incarnations throughout your life:

Cute baby hair

Chances are, unless you were one of the ones that stayed bald as an egg till you were five, you had soft curling tendrils of beautiful, perfect, healthy hair when you were a small human. You don't have to do anything with baby hair; maybe add a cute bow or clip it out of their little eyes so they only spend 50% of their time falling over and walking into things. There is no such thing as a Bad Hair Day for a baby; even if it's stuck to the side of their face with drool or chocolate, or sticking up every which way after a nap, they're still as adorable as a bag full of puppies.

'My parents hate me!'

This stage usually comes around about school time. There is the sudden rush to 'tidy up' and make kids look respectable and less like one of Tarzan's offspring, before they are shipped off to hang out with the other pristine, immaculate children. What is the answer? The Fringe, of course! That ubiquitous childhood hair that we all sported, in various degrees of Bowl Cut. And, if like me you grew up in the 80s, there was The Mullet. The least said about that, the better. I think we should move on before we all start retiring to the corners, to rock gently and sob over those old, hideous school photos.

Teenage rebellion

Now, this is more like it. You finally have an identity and an attitude, and you have realised that actually it is YOUR hair and you can do what you want with it! And, there is nothing your parents can do about it! Yes, they can tremulously tell you that it might not be such a good idea to cover your entire head in bleach three days in a row, trying to achieve your Nordic friend's level of blond. They can protest all they like about the shaved patches which, in the right light and from the right angle, look a little bit like your favourite rock star. They may have something to say about the fact that the bathroom is now liberally splattered with various shades of rainbow coloured, semi permanent hair dye – but they can't stop you! And woe betide them if they try, you mutter to yourself as you march out of the door, safe in the knowledge that your new hair looks GREAT.

20s sensibleness

This stage fairly closely follows the previous one. This is the time when you quietly shelve the tacky colours and godawful cuts of your youth, and try desperately to reclaim the health of the hair that you once took so for granted, before you permanently ruined it by burning it right down into the follicles with your cheap bleach. You may have a job by now, and be able to afford to pay someone else to cut your hair rather than relying on Mum giving it a 'bit of a tidy up'. Your hair suddenly takes over your life. You have regular salon appointments, you buy all the equipment to make it curlier, straighter, sleeker, healthier; you treat it to hair masks and take supplements to make it even glossier. This is your hair's heyday – make the most of it.

30s 'Ah, feck it'

You still have hair, it's still in fairly good condition, you don't feel tempted to do crazy things with it in order to explore different parts of your character. (You've explored your character a fair bit; you don't think you're going to be the next Bowie or Blondie, so you don't need to worry too much about your mop.) You may have had a baby, and been lulled into a false sense of security by the hormones that make your barnet gorgeous and glossy – then stopped caring, as you realised you'll never have time to brush your hair again, let alone wash it. Regular salon trips slip into once a year territory, where all they can do is hack off your split ends and beg you to come back for maintenance before another 365 days have passed. You promise faithfully, crossing your fingers behind your back.

40s onwards

Now, we head back into Sensible Territory, but with less of the obsessiveness of the 20s. You probably pay slightly more attention to your hair that before, as you are becoming alarmingly aware that it is the one part of your body that is not actively falling apart. You gaily cover up the greys – but subtly, so that everyone comments on your 'natural' look and congratulate you on escaping the ravages of Father Time. You then go home and sob over your box of Cover Them Greys, feeling like a total fraud.

50s plus

You have probably, by this point, realised that the whole world and everything in it does not actually fall apart if your hair doesn't look as though you have just stepped out of Toni And Guy's. You may have started to embrace the Silver Fox look, and with any luck you have passed the awkward 'growing it out' phase, where you look like a motheaten badger. Most days you're just grateful that you still have hair.

For boys, these stages are pretty much: **Baby. Sensible. Gone**

Skin

Despite the fact that this is actually the body's largest organ, it is one of the most badly treated of all.[180] We neglect it, expose it to radiation that will eventually leave it as haggard and wrinkled as a leather sofa in a busy coffee shop, scrub it with harsh towels when we should be gently patting it dry, and neglect to drink enough water thus leaving it dehydrated and sunken.

No one thinks about skin when they're young, do they? That's because we're all dewy and fresh-faced, and still filled with collagen. You might have a period in teenagerhood where you are so ravaged with spots it looks like you are permanently dressed in your Hallowe'en makeup, but this usually passes.

Then, all of a sudden – generally around mid 20s – you spot that first telltale wrinkle. It doesn't keep you up at night; after all, smile lines are a sign that you have a happy, fulfilled life exploding with joy and giggles, right? But hang on. What's that line between your eyebrows? Surely that wasn't there before? And what about those little marks appearing around your mouth? Seriously, what is the function of all these useless additions to our once-bright, smooth skin?

In my opinion, it is to prevent the older generation from accidentally procreating, because the only people who can bear to look at a face full of wrinkles are other people who also have a face full of wrinkles, and are thus unable to effectively reproduce.

Well, actually, I don't think this at all. Ageing is a natural part of life, and while I'm not saying that you should spend the rest of the time drinking strong coffee instead of water, and wandering about in 50 degree heat without any suncream, you should try to just accept that this is something that inevitably happens to us

---

[180] Apart from the liver. Obviously.

all.[181] Getting old and wrinkly is actually a great privilege, when you think about it. There are a frightening number of people who don't make it to the appropriate age for developing wrinkles, so each and every one of those lines can be seen as a gift from life. You don't have to like them, obviously, and feel free to spend your life savings on treatments and lotions to reduce the signs of ageing – but don't feel too bad about it.

Roald Dahl[182] wrote a wonderful quote which has stuck with me for the whole of my life, ever since I first read The Twits. It goes:

'If you have good thoughts, they will shine out of your face like sunbeams, and you will always look lovely.'

Obviously he was not saying that you won't look as wrinkly as an old prune, and that your teeth will all still be present and correct by the time you are 80 – but actually he is totally right. If you are a lovely being, it really will ooze out through your pores and you will always be considered beautiful. Hopefully you will consider yourself beautiful too, as you will realise that the true value that should be placed on any person is how much light they bring to the world, not how smooth their forehead is.

Body Shape

This is a particularly tricky one. Unfortunately we have all been brainwashed by society to think that there is only one type of body shape that is acceptable, and if you do not quite fit into this box[183] then you should be cast out of society and left outside in the cold with the other outcasts, staring longingly into the windows of the party where all the Beautiful People are.

The thing is, this ideal body shape tends to change with time, and from culture to culture. For example, in medieval times in England, the Ideal Body was covered with enough blubber to make a baby whale jealous, because this denoted that you were rich and important enough to not actually do any work, and could spend all your time eating. This was a time when people generally started work at around 2 and a half, and didn't stop till they died, which was around 30.

These days, having a physique akin to a racing snake crossed with a greyhound is what we're all after – and once again, it denotes riches.

---

[181]   Unless you die. I mean, that is literally the only other option.
[182]   Who should also be known as God.
[183]   Or through a doorway.

You can afford to buy only organic food and you have a personal trainer who comes to your house to pummel you into shape.

You go for weekly back massages and the lady at the facial salon knows you and your skin type like the back of her (perfectly manicured) hand.

You follow any number of fad diets that promise you body perfection for a princely fee, and you change your preferences depending on what Gwyneth Paltrow is currently touting.

You can subtly and discreetly nip and tuck and lift, then breezily explain to everyone that your shape is all down to the fact that you drink only the finest apple cider vinegar, squeezed from the Apples of Life by the toned thighs of virgins. Oh yes, it's pretty easy to stay in good shape when you have this army of helpers behind you.

There is something far more important than looking like a supermodel, especially if you don't have the right genes that will allow you to do so, and that is: being healthy and happy.

The thing is, we all have parts of ourselves that we feel could be smaller/bigger/less jiggly/more toned – but even these less than perfect parts of your body are all working together to allow you to move around, talk, sing, dance, enjoy your hobbies and generally survive in the world.

Don't hate your thick thighs, they can power you up a mountain faster than that little stick insect.

Instead of loathing your arms for their spindliness, be thankful that you can pick things up without having to spend hours at the gym like your massive friend.

If your tummy is bigger than you want it to be, who cares? It means you're far more likely to be sat on by someone's cat, or cuddled by children when they have fallen over.

So you're a bit short. All this means is that you can hide in the crowd better when the Zombie Apocalypse strikes, leaving all the tall ones to be eaten first.

Boobs too big/too small? Never mind. Remind yourself that they were functional before they were sexual, and no matter how big or small or lopsided, you will still be able to feed your babies.

Confidence is a great thing. It is wonderful for your self image, and for the way everyone else looks at you. A great thing about confidence is that you can actually fake it – not like the time that you took to the stage and thought you'd bash out a bit of Adele – and it will actually start to become a part of you. I'm not saying you should go around shouting that you are god's gift, but practising confidence in your every day life and trying to pretend you don't care what other people think, you may start to find that you actually don't.

It turns out that the only opinion that matters when it comes to your body, your face, your hair – in fact any aspect of your life – is YOUR opinion. You are the only one that matters when it comes to you, so as long as you are happy then screw everyone else.[184]

A fun thing to do is to stick little post it notes around your house in places where you will see them, with life affirming phrases or sayings on them. Your friends will all think you've finally lost the plot, and it may interfere with your flamingo feature wall, but these good things will ooze their way into your psyche, and can actually help you feel happier, more confident and generally happier and more comfortable with your body and your life.

If you want to exercise to lose a bit of chub, go for it. If you want to make your body more toned, excellent! Just remember to celebrate yourself and your achievements, and remember that being happy is much better than being thin. When the Zombie Apocalypse hits, it would be good to have a bit of extra insulation to keep you going until you've established a community and started growing your own veggies, right?

Look after your body as if it was your favourite pet; feed it good foods, tuck it up to sleep with a blanket and lots of love; exercise it and give it lots of belly rubs. Look in the mirror every day and tell yourself that you're perfect – because you really, truly are.

Accepting your body and your appearance is, according to those Buddhist types who always seem serene and peaceful, all you need to do in order to not have to stress about it for the rest of time. However, for most of us, 'accepting our body' is a great excuse to eat all the pies, and never concern ourselves with our own personal happiness or focus on the reasons why we want to eat all the pies in the first place.

I think what we should all do is just be more accepting. We should realise that we are all people, with different Things and different views on life – basically, if you like it, buy it a coffee. If you don't, move on.

If you don't like yourself, buy yourself a coffee anyway, and move on. Realise that your body, although it may have bits that are not as good/big/small as your

---

184   Not literally. We're not actually suggesting you do this.

97

best mate's ones, is your very own, and it is perfect and beautiful. There's a great quote I know[185] that goes:

'Even slugs, you know, are much admired by other slugs.'

This one got me thinking. Ok, so I may be a bit hideous, and I may very much dislike certain wobbly bits, and feel infinitely inferior to just about anyone else I ever meet – but what if they are all feeling like that too? After all, no one talks about their feelings much do they? What if we're ALL slugs of one type or another, waiting to find out very own slug?

What if (shock horror) every single body type was acceptable by society, and magazines and media did not only portray The Beautiful[186] among us? Perhaps that would give us less unrealistic ideals – for example, if your father is 4 foot 2 and your mother is a pocket sized pixie, chances are you won't grow up to be a 6 foot supermodel.

But, despite your lack of supermodel status, if you could manage to accept your beautiful, functioning, goddamn GORGEOUS body for what it was and what it does for you, wouldn't you be much happier?[187]

---

[185] It came from an audio book of *Orlando The Marmalade Cat,* in case you're interested. Oracles can come from many places.

[186] This ideal, by the way, has changed a squillion times throughout the course of history, and varies from country to country. Beauty is subjective? Who knew?!

[187] When you figure out how to do this, let me know please. More therapy on the way.

Food

Despite the fact that this stuff is literally just fuel that keeps us alive, we don't 'arf have a funny relationship with it, don't we? Most of us eat too much. Some of us deliberately eat not enough. A horrifying amount of us CAN'T eat enough, due to the craziness of today's society.[188] Some of us eat for fun, some of us eat for necessity, some of us don't really think about it all that much. Some of us hate certain things; some of us explode if we eat certain things; some of us feel life is not worth living without certain things.[189]

---

[188] See 'Money' and 'Politics'.

[189] Blue cheese and sweet chilli sauce, anyone?? *Really, Miss Hancock! I deplore the duplication of question marks. Think of the countless forests being despoiled to accommodate your excesses.*

Food is a big subject. Really, all it is is a means to keep us alive – but if you delve into it deeper, there are better and worse things that you can be putting into your body.[190]

When you think about it, astronaut food is actually the best thing that we can all be eating. It is a carefully balanced blend of all the right nutrients, vitamins and minerals that we need to keep our bodies functioning optimally, and all you need to do is add some hot water.

However.

This would be a bit rubbish. Food, it turns out, is actually so much more than food.

'Break bread with me' doesn't just mean 'Come in and nibble on my old, stale loaf,'[191] but 'Enter my home and we will share hospitality and friendship'. Cooking deliciousness for friends and family is one of the nicest things you can do – even if all this involves is opening a few bags of crisps and passing the nuts around.[192]

Eating stuff, in this day and age, can be tricky. Many more people seem to have allergies to various different things – I imagine such allergies used to exist in Ye Old Days, but then the possessors of such allergies would pretty much just die quite quickly. These days we have a lot more diagnostic tools at our disposal, plus the means to make things that people aren't allergic to, equalling less death.

Food is a comforting thing; a fun thing; a socialising thing; a bonding thing. It is infinitely better if you enjoy it, but even if you don't you should still do it, because of the whole Staying Alive thing.

It would be good if we all ate the things that were actually good for us, instead of popping down to Maccas when we feel a bit peckish. Jamie Oliver was right – this stuff really is NOT food. It is so filled with chemicals and preservatives that it will literally never rot. Fast food is great, but you're far better off with a greasy spoon sandwich than a MacDonald's burger – at least you know the greasy spoon food doesn't contain more chemicals than Pete Docherty.

Trouble is, a healthy diet can seem considerably less appealing than a dirty burger. Who wants a plate full of salad when you can have a plateful of tasty calories, dripping with cheese and juicy fat? But, you know, in this day and age you can have some really yummy, delicious food that is also good for you. You can even have the ingredients delivered to your door, with a handy little recipe card, for goodness sake! There really is very little excuse...

---

[190] [Snigger] Some of those things won't actually keep you alive, though.

[191] [Snigger]

[192] I reckon I can manage a snigger at this, too.

...Oh no, wait, there is. Food that is awful for you is SO much cheaper than the good stuff. It is very hard to eat healthily if you are on a tiny budget, as so many of us are. Why on EARTH is organic food more expensive than non organic? Surely they would have saved loads on pesticides, so it should be loads cheaper, right? Why on EARTH do we import thousands of products from abroad, adding not only to their cost but to the issues faced by our planet? Wouldn't it be better to eat food that is grown in this country? Can't we bulldoze every single McDonalds and replace them with community gardens, where people can join in growing fruits and vegetables and help themselves to the produce?

No matter how you look at it, food is a source of power, as well as the health and Staying Alive thing. It starts in childhood – if you decide you won't eat it, literally no one can force you. And if they do, you have the power to regurgitate it all over the soft furnishings. This is one of the first things children do to exercise their right to bodily autonomy. This should be celebrated, of course – but, the little bastards take it too far.

I have a friend who relates a tale of his childhood, where he went through a period of refusing any food apart from chips, sausages and beans. Desperate, his mother took him to the doctor. This wise old man prescribed a treatment of feeding the child nothing but chips, sausages and beans, and confidently predicted he would choose something else once the novelty wore off. Can you guess what happened? That's right. He happily munched his way through platefuls of potatoes, pigs and pulses until his mother tore her hair out and refused to feed them to him any more. He was hungry for a bit, then realised that he too had to stay alive.

I remember being Small and Grumpy, and taking agin' having peas on my plate during one Sunday dinner at Grandma's house. They were quickly removed from my plate. This was a revelation. Suddenly I didn't have to eat them! Ohhh, the power my small self had! It backfired slightly, because I actually quite liked peas. I maintained my dignity by refusing to eat any form of pea unless it was frozen, until I got old and realised I didn't have to keep up the pretence any more.

The people who have the food wield the power. This has been the case since the peasant times, so it is no wonder that the majority of us, once we move out on our own, have no filter whatsoever when it comes to the weekly shop. Luckily, financial issues[193] prevent us from spending every single penny we have on crap food that makes us feel pants and contributes to our issues.

---

[193] See 'Money' and 'Politics'

We do, eventually, realise that we have to eat something other than chips and pasta in order to maintain a body that functions and doesn't resemble a potato. We buy fancy cook books and picture ourselves, rosy with health, presiding over a huge scrubbed table surrounded by happy munching sounds, as our loved ones feast on our lovingly prepared meals. What generally happens is we accidentally set fire to said cookbook and decide that serving it, along with a side salad, will be tastier and more nutritious than the meal we were trying to cook from it.

It's a sign of a lucky society, if you have the time, inclination and money to pick all sorts of different diets that might improve your health or your appearance, isn't it? We are fortunate these days that we don't have to hunt for our food, and that we can buy all sorts of out of season fruits and vegetables in supermarkets. Those that can't afford caviar have to scrabble about in the food banks for a lonely packet of stale Cornflakes.

There is actually enough food in the world, and enough wealth for said food, to buy each and every one of us at least one square meal a day – in fact, supermarkets throw away the equivalent of football pitch sized piles of food every week. We really need to sort out our wastefulness, and enjoy the luxury that is eating.

If you have allergies that prevent you eating certain things then I'm very sorry. I'm not trying to be offensive, just funny. Just be thankful that you live in These Days rather than Them Days, when your allergies would have killed you before you got a chance to read this and write me a letter saying You're Just Not Funny.

Now, let's look into the various different diets, in a hilarious type way that may just have you sobbing into your Buscopan:

- **Standard** – You like food, you can eat just about all of it without exploding, though there are bound to be some things you don't like. You'll pretty much give anything a go, from stir-fried crickets to a blue steak, safe in the knowledge that you are happy with your dietary choices and nothing you eat is going to make you break out in hives. Pass on the artichokes though.[194]

- **Vegetarian** – You don't like to eat dead stuff, either from a moral point of view or the fact you just don't enjoy the taste. You tend to go for the standard veggie option in a pub, and silently thank the world that things have moved on from a blank stare and an offer of a cheese sandwich into which they will probably insert ham, because they feel sorry for you.[195] You

---

[194]   You're not alone. Most sensible people do.
[195]   This actually happened to me.

have learned to roll your eyes at the 'rabbit food' jokes, and chuckle politely when a Standard eater offers you a stick of celery. Oh, the hilarity.

- **Pescatarian** – You don't want to to hurt wildlife, you really don't, so you avoid meat products. You believe in the sentience of all the beings and not being cruel to stuff – but fish, surely, are ok? They don't have nervous systems, do they? This means you get at least one more option in a pub than your standard Veggie, and you can console yourself that at least it's good for your body,[196] and tell yourself that the fish probably don't mind too much.

- **Vegan** – Vegans are the best of people, they really are. You may have been put off by a particularly militant one (and there are a lot of them) but basically vegans are concerned about other sentient beings. Making sure we don't kill other creatures is drummed into us since childhood, isn't it? So, no wonder some people decide to take this to its furthest extremes. Many won't even drive through towns with Ham in the name.[197]

- **Coeliac** – You can eat just about anything apart from wheat. Wheat will instantly make you explode in all sorts of unpleasant ways. There is a theory that it's not actually the wheat itself but the cocktail of chemicals in which it is drenched before it arrives on our plates that causes the issues, but either way you won't be ordering a cheese sandwich any time soon.

- **Low histamine** – This is a new-ish issue that seems to be striking a proportion of the population. Anything with histamine in it will make you explode, so you avoid it. Sadly, most foods seem to have this elusive little thing,[198] so your diet is as bland as a fasting monks' and you're absolutely no fun at dinner parties.

- **Keto** – In the interests of your health, you pretty much eat nothing but meat. You have to be fairly rich in order to do this, unless you run a farm and butcher your own animals. You also become pretty boring, and people glaze over when talking to you as you spend much of your time working out percentages of carbs and fats and various different things you need to do in order to trick your body into eating up all its fat reserves.

---

[196] Looking at the levels of crap in our seas though, and the dreadful ways we fish the creatures that live in it, this option is almost certainly not good for your body.

[197] This is not my hilarity. Bill Bailey, you are also God.

[198] What the hell even is histamine? If you know, do send me a little letter about it.

- **Palaeo** – This is the type of diet practised by people who are nostalgic for the days when we lived in caves, hunted for our food and went 'Ug' a lot. It's basically meat, fish, nuts and things, the sort of thing our cave person ancestors would have eaten. However, you are allowed to cook it all with fancy sauces and tasty additions, rather than tearing the flesh from the bones. You don't have to say Ug in order to follow this diet, but we've been told it helps.

- **Raw food** – Cooking in all its forms is the killer of all the wonderful nutrients that food provides us with,[199] so you will only eat raw things. This generally doesn't extend to meat, although some do, possibly in an attempt to get in touch with our prehistoric roots or possibly because of latent suicidal tendencies and a desire to vomit a lot. If you are on this diet because of hippy-type tendencies, you may take it once step further and only eat fruit that has fallen from the tree. You'll be pretty hungry in the winter.

---

[199]   This is not true, just so you know.

Hobbies

You remember these things, right? When you were small they took up an awful lot of your time, because you had no other responsibilities and all the time in the world. Plus, you had devoted people who were willing to not only pay for your hobbies but ferry you halfway around the countryside to attend them. I miss those days.

As you get older, you may still try to do your hobbies, but as the gap between finishing work and bedtime gets smaller and smaller, it is very hard to fit in anything Fun at all. If you're lucky you might grab half an hour once a month to finish painting your Warhammer figures, or read that novel – but generally

Hobbies go by the wayside as you get older, to be replaced with Work and Sleep. Sad times.

Hobbies are often something you are good at, or trying to become good at, or things that you are no good at but you still enjoy.[200] Any and all of these things are great reasons for doing something for your very own self – and they can be literally anything you like! Because you are generally not paid to do these things, unless you are lucky enough to have a hobby that you are good enough at and that other people want to get involved in enough, it doesn't actually matter how dedicated you are to them or how much time you actually manage to spend on them.

Reading

One of the cheapest and easiest hobbies there are, reading is something that can be enjoyed by everyone. There is literally just about any genre you are into; from crime and autobiography to unicorn porn maintenance and serious, thought provoking philosophy. Reading is great because you can sit on your bum, tell everyone else to do one, and create an entire fantasy world in your head which is, in many cases, far more fun and much more interesting than the one you are actually inhabiting.

Writing

This is a wonderful hobby (I would say that, wouldn't I?). You can make up wonderful fantasy worlds which are, in many cases, far more fun and much more interesting than the one that you are currently inhabiting. Or, you can waste an inordinate amount of time trying to write a funny book that will make people laugh and hopefully make you a lot of money. Both of these things remain to be seen.

Drawing

Art is a fantastic thing. It can be moving, inspirational, exciting, thought provoking and it can also be really good therapy. From 'drawing the grumpy monster' as a child, to working through various life traumas later on after the event, art is

---

[200]   See 'Sex'.

wonderful. Ever since the first of our ancestors dipped their hands in ochre clay and discovered that they could make a mark on a rock, then 'Ug!''d excitedly to their friends, art has been a way of communicating and of making ourselves heard, for thousands of years. Apparently, even pickling a shark is considered Art these days, so your mandalas created by spitting ketchup onto a sheet are totally valid.

Music

Another marvellous art form! You can include music as your hobby whether you enjoy making it or listening to it,[201] and both can be equally rewarding. Some people can make money out of their music; some people make money out of it even if they are not widely considered to be any good.[202][203] If you are No Good at music, maybe keeping it as a hobby is the best idea... Unless you are No Good at the violin, the bagpipes or the drums. Anyone who is No Good at these things should definitely NOT be allowed it as a hobby. And, while we're on the subject, if your hobby is jazz, in any of its forms, please throw this book away and consider placing your head into a hot oven, for quite some time, until common sense kicks in.

Painting

Making the world more colourful is always a good idea, isn't it? After all, we've come a long way from the days when you could only make red by squishing beetles, and a certain type of blue was more expensive than all the riches of all kings in all the world. Whether you like oils, watercolours, acrylics or that other one beginning with G that no one can pronounce, painting is a fantastic way to pass the time. There are a great many things you can paint; from designs that come from your own mind to colouring in handy little designs that someone else has made. Painting small, fantastical creatures or historical armies is also growing massively in popularity, and this is also a valid form of artwork. Don't let anyone tell you it's not – just point them in the direction of those films they really like to watch and they'll soon change their tunes.

---

[201] As long as you don't become one of those people who sneer at other people's music choices. No one needs that.

[202] Do not say Bono. Do not say Bono. Do not say Bono.

[203] I really like U2. Sorry guys.

Walking

Although this is a funny thing to have as a hobby – after all, walking is generally our main means of getting about, and you wouldn't say you're indulging your hobbies if you are simply walking to work – it is also really cool. You can see some amazing things when you ditch the car and use your legs – plus there's the added bonus of getting outside, fresh air, getting a bit fitter, and all that good jazz.[204] Some people take it to serious extremes and buy fancy kit in order to Go Walking – there is a huge industry for boots, coats, backpacks, water bottles, and sticks. Ever heard of Nordic Walking? This is ordinary walking, but the enjoyers of it get to carry around pointy sticks. Maybe it's some kind of hark back to our caveman days? Who knows.

Dancing

Most of us are born with the ability to move our bodies around, although this ability decreases with age (see Health). If you get going at it young enough, you can be one of those people who can REALLY move their bodies around, in all sorts of seriously impressive ways. If not, you should definitely still caper around your kitchen in a primeval way once in a while. It's great fun.

Making Things

This is a huge category, as there are just a squillion and one things you can make. Little wooden toys, cupboards, clay models, socks, a massive mess – the huge list just keeps on going.

Carving things out of wood or stone is one of our oldest art forms, and were probably as great hobbies for cave people (when they weren't all busy trying to survive tiger attacks and dealing with the privations of living in a cave and not having supermarkets) as they are for us today.

Creating clothing is another astonishing skill – crocheters and knitters can weave astonishing garments using just a bit of wool and a needle or two, while those that make stuff out of actual Stuff[205] are also to be celebrated. Never mind that it costs arms and legs more to home-make your garments than it does to buy

---

[204] There is no good jazz, just so we're clear.
[205] Old fashioned word for material. Yes, I'm just showing off now.

them – but come the Zombie Apocalypse we'll be very glad of these people, once all the poor sweat shop workers have had their brains eaten.

Foraging

This is a 'new' hobby that has actually been around for as long as humanity has. Foraging used to literally be the equivalent of popping to the shops, so I don't understand why it's suddenly considered to be the cool thing to do. Don't get me wrong, I'm all for getting people out and about into nature, and realising what wonderful things and resources we have at our fingertips. The problem is that most people are idiots. There are a great many groups set up to help you discover what is tasty and what will poison you, so for god's sake get some ideas before you create a delicious meal featuring Death Caps and invite Aunt Ethel over.

Cooking

A great hobby if you like to eat. Actually, also a great hobby if you don't like to eat – there will always be someone near you who does like to eat, unless your cooking is horrible. If it is, I'd advise a good cookbook, or a different hobby.

Gaming

I rather object to this use of the word. It traditionally means gambling.[206]

This is probably the most common thing that people would list as their hobby these days. Like reading, it involves quite a lot of sitting on one's bum, but possibly with a little less of the imagination being stimulated. However, it has been said that people can become very good pilots because of having spent their formative years quite literally twiddling their thumbs... Not sure I'd feel safe being flown about by someone who is used to throwing down the controller and wandering off in search of something to eat though.

There's one thing I find weirder about Gaming than anything else... It's the fascination with watching videos of other people gaming. Seriously, what is that about? You're not playing it, it's a bit boring, and you might as well be watching

---

206   I couldn't agree more, Miss Hancock; it is a foolish misappropriation of the word.

telly. Or reading a book. Or writing one. Or drawing a picture. Or enjoying music. Or... Pretty much anything else really.[207]

---

[207]   This is why Young People don't like me.

Sport

We thought we'd have a whole separate section for sports, even though they are technically hobbies, because they are something that people get very hot under the collar about. It's the same concept as Politics and Religion – it's basically an excuse to sit in a comfortable tribe and wave pointy sticks threateningly at The Other Lot.

Sport has been around for a very long time, since the first days that humankind thought they would flex their muscles or their running skills and make other humans look bad because they were so much better at it. It is basically just a bunch of people running around, sitting, bending over, whacking things with other things, jumping over things, throwing things a long way in the air, kicking things or riding things, within a very specific set of rules entirely to try and do it better than another set of people that are doing the same thing. For the people doing it it makes sense, it's good, healthy fun. For everyone else it should be entirely meaningless. But, it isn't.

Gladiators had it about right, didn't they? Place a small, weak human who has been starved and beaten into a ring with a bronzed, muscled Adonis of a human, and watch the outcome. It turns out we're pretty bloodthirsty, when it comes down to it.

People gather to watch their group of people attempt to beat the other group of people. They pay a lot of money to be there. They sing and chant and applaud and boo and hug and cry about whether their chosen group of people proves better at the Thing than the others.

They don't even know these people. They will likely never meet these people and these people are probably getting paid in a week what they get paid in a lifetime to do something that is, in fact entirely pointless. It makes no sense. But yet, I am one of these people. I love sport. Virtually any sport.[208] I watch it with my friends and enjoy every second, and that's what it's all about. It's not about your group being better than theirs. It's about being in your gang and cheering them on. It's tribalism, its base, and that's why it really gets you in the feels.

The festivals around the big sporting events, such as football's World Cup or the Olympics, are incredible. The melding together of so many different races and cultures, foods and clothes, all brought together by a love of one simple (and let's face it, pointless) Thing is inspiring, and really is an example of humans at their best and the best of humans.

For most, the love of the sport allows fans to forget differences and relish the fact that they all have this one thing in common. It is a wonderful dichotomy that such mutual respect can be created through a game that, at its heart, is about beating the Other Lot.

Sport, in its purest form, is a wonderful thing. It gets us outdoors, running around and being all cardiovascular-y. However, many of us prefer to not actually take part, but to shout at the ones that are taking part, and getting our pointy sticks out if someone else doesn't like the particular Sport that we like. And, god forbid if someone else prefers the opposite team of our chosen Sport! That's when the pointy sticks really come into their own, and actual injuries can occur.

There are some that ruin it. There are thugs and hooligans that are only there for violence and hate. But they are not the true fans. It is often this horrid 5% that get all the headlines, because hate sells, and that is a shame because sport is

---

[208]   Although the nuances of women's beach volleyball are particularly mesmerising.

one of the few things that shows that our differences can be, instead of disliked, applauded through a mutual love.

We're going to have a look at a few Sports in greater detail – now, we know there are a lot of them, and we'll almost certainly miss out on a few. If we have missed out your favourite one, buy a copy of this book for all your friends and family and we promise we'll include it in the sequel.

Football

Everyone loves football.[209] Even if you're not a footy fan and you don't even bat an eyelid when the team from your home town are playing a match, you probably wouldn't mind if we had another bank holiday because we actually won something. This game evolved from a bunch of kids kicking around an inflated pig's bladder (yes, really), and it's evolved into one of the biggest money spinners in the entire world. Seriously, the money that these guys make could end world hunger within a few months.[210] They dash about, looking cool and funky, then fall over in a big massive heap if someone from the other team breathes on them. Violence is incited in the supporters, who can deal with far worse injuries than the actual footballers do. But, for some reason, there is something mesmerising about this sport. It may be solely the pride that one feels when one finally understands the Offside Rule, who knows.

Rugby

Ah, now we're talking. Burly men running around in little shorts, displaying athleticism and strength and utter stoicism – have you seen what happens when those guys get hurt? They may lie down on the pitch for a minute or two to let the concussion kick in, then they're up again with the blood streaming down their jerseys and four of their teeth missing. This is truly the Beautiful Game.[211] It's literally cave man stuff.[212] Plus, there is the advantage of occasionally getting to

---

209   In that, Miss Hancock, you are sorely mistaken. I detest football with every fibre of my being. – And me too!

210   Marcus Rashford, we worship you. I hope you are not intending to include me in that absurd assertion!

211   It's not actually all that beautiful though, is it? The cauliflower ears, the broken noses, the eyes looking in different directions because of all the blows to the head… It's a good job they're good at what they do.

212   There is something in what you say, Miss Hancock. At my school, if there were insufficient pupils to make up two full sides, we'd play Stonehenge Rugby; the only rule was that no weapons would be used. It was a suitably troglodytic experience.

watch the Haka. Ohhh, how we love the Haka. Brings tears to my eyes and a chill up my spine, every single time.

Cricket

Literally no one understands this, yet it is one of the most widely played game across the globe. People get very het up about those little sticks that the players have to knock over, and they are hilarious in their white trousers with enough body protection to prevent a wild boar attack. To be fair, a cricket ball is made of compressed volcano ash mixed with lead, covered with the skin of long-dead ancestors,[213] so you really don't want it smashing you in the head. There is some running around, a lot of standing around, and the most exciting bit is watching the bowler perform all those crazy acrobatics before he actually throws the ball.

Tennis

The best bit about tennis[214] is all the noises. They howl like people carrying really heavy loads, don't they? To be fair, the players do pack a hefty punch. Those serve speeds can rival Concorde, and they generally have great big muscles. The most fun part about any tennis match is watching the star have a tantrum and fling his racquet into the crowd, but even when this doesn't happen, watching two or four people bash a ball around, grunting loudly, is not the worst way to spend an afternoon. Unless you have a bit of drying-out paint that needs an eye keeping on it.

Swimming

In my humble opinion, swimming is an absolute necessity. Who knows when the sea might suddenly decide to engulf the earth, and we'll all have to make it to high ground somehow? Swimming for pleasure is a wonderful thing; swimming for necessity is an essential thing. Swimming for glory is... Also pretty awesome, really. Remember trying to learn the Butterfly stroke? There was probably one kid in your school who could do it, and this kid was always looked up to as a god. They generally had massive shoulders, and always smelled faintly of chlorine.

---

[213] There is no part of this description which bears any resemblance to the truth.

[214] Apart from the girls in little skirts scratching their bums.

Watching people swimming around in search of medals is pretty cool, despite the fact that they all look like condoms with goggles on.

Cycling

Surely, this is the most boring of sports. It would be more fun if they cycled through dangerous terrain, having to battle bears and tigers and things, but generally these guys just ride around a Velodrome, looking bored and aerodynamic. The Tour De France got a bit more exciting a while ago, when it was discovered that the best rider ever was only so good because he was buzzing on an illegal cocktail of things that made him artificially better than everyone else, but since then things have gone a bit quiet. Apart from that time someone was holding up a sign showing their love and support for the riders, and proceeded to take out the entire race[215] with it. Ahh, good times.

Boxing

This is one of the most primitive forms of sport. Blokes[216] punching each other until one or other of them passes out, while people bet money on which one of them will spit out blood and teeth first. Not a good thing to watch if you don't like blood, or the image of people sprawling on the floor surrounded by their teeth. They do seem to spend a lot of their time hugging, which may make you think they quite like each other – but refer back to the pre-match posturing, and you'll realise that this is not the case.

Gymnastics

What a wonderful thing! Look at what these contortionists can do with their bodies! Gymnastics really is incredible to watch, despite the fact that it makes you feel like the fattest, laziest lump of humanity as you slob around on the sofa watching these people who are literally at the peak of their physical fitness do things that make your eyes water. This feeling is exacerbated when you get up for another biscuit and fall to the floor in a heap as your back gives out.

---

[215]   Just the cyclists, not the whole human race, thankfully.

[216]   We let the ladies do it now, too. Do keep up.

Ice Skating

This is really the pinnacle of all sports, isn't it? Beautiful people in spangly, revealing costumes, twirling around on the ice in a combination of dancing and flying. The generally have cool music to do their thang to as well, which adds to the appeal. Another great thing is that you can sit on the edge of your seat, waiting with baited breath until one of them drops the other and they land in a heap of crestfallen misery on the frozen surface, while everyone winces and remembers that time they nearly sliced off someone's fingers at the local ice rink.

Equestrian

Horses, whether or not you are a fan of them, are actually pretty cool. They are enormous, semi wild creatures, who have been tamed enough to handle being ridden around – but they have the added excitement of occasionally going mental, for no reason. We're not going to talk about racing at all, because this a barbaric practise that ruins both many horses, and many people's lives. But, showjumping! Cross country! Dressage! Most people's experience of dressage, unless you are involved with horses, comes from the 2012 Olympics, where Britain swept the boards with dancing horses that took the entire world by storm. Dressage is actually quite hard work, despite the fact that it looks like they are just skipping through the forest glades. 10/10.

Politics

No matter what you feel about politics, they are going to be a big part of your life. You may think that the baying mob in Westminster don't actually have that much impact on your life, but the chilling truth is… They really, really do.

Laws that are passed in Parliament affect your daily rights, so it is actually pretty darn important that you read about the different policies and educate yourself on what party does what, and how these things can affect your own particular life. Yes, I know it's boring, and yes, I know you have better things to do with your time – but actually, when you think about it, casually handing all of your power over to a bunch of toffs out of touch with the world you live in is pretty much the worst idea that you can have.

Back in the days when political parties first started appearing {insert intelligent research about when political parties first started appearing},[217] the peasants were completely exempt from having one single iota of a say in anything. You simply kept your head down, tugged your forelock, feasted on your turnips and hoped that the lord of the manor decided not to kill you or your children that day.

Nowadays, we actually have a chance to make things different.

Did you know that the politicians you elect are actually there to serve you, and make your life better? I bet you didn't. It took me ages to figure this out. These people are not gods; they do not deserve their 80k a year salary, especially because, in general, they don't make anyone's life any better. In fact, some political parties when they come to power will actually make your life considerably worse.[218]

The thing is, we have the power to change the political future of our country. We do not (yet) live in a dictatorship, and we can choose to oust one political party if we so choose. The thing is though, we actually have to CHOOSE. I cannot stress this enough.

If you are old enough to vote, VOTE. If you are not old enough to vote, badger the people around you. If you are jaded and cynical and don't see the point of anything – I feel you, I really do. But still, VOTE.

This is the only way that we can do anything to change our existence.

...Well, actually, that's a bit of a misleading statement. There is a lot more we can do to change our existence. Start by:

- Realising that you and you alone have complete control over your life. If you don't like a particular policy, write to your MP; lobby for change; glue parts of your body to major roads.

- Vote

- Refuse to accept the things that they tell you. I might add again – the braying mob in Westminster is here to serve YOU, not the other way around.

- Vote!

- Lobby for a different voting system, whereby your actual vote will actually count as a thumbs up to your favourite candidate.[219]

---

[217] Yes, I really do wish you would introduce intelligent research about something, Miss Hancock.

[218] Cough, cough, TORIES, cough. I don't know how that one slipped through, Miss Hancock. I thought I had censored everything in sight.

[219] Proportional Representation is the word you are looking for. Be careful what you ask for, Young Lady. In the 2015 general election, your beloved SNP won 56 seats at Westminster with 4.7% of the vote,

- Vote.

Although it may seem pointless, because in this country we have a stupid system that means you voting for one political party you like does not ACTUALLY represent one vote for said party, you still have to vote.

We are a bit pathetic in this country, to be honest. No one bothers to turn out to the voting booths; they're always on a Thursday and usually held during the most miserable weather that you can imagine, and you don't want to queue for hours in the drizzle, especially because you are guaranteed to run into Aunt Ethel, who insists on going to vote because she might run into someone she knows, despite the fact that she can't even see the boxes to tick let alone the names of the politicians next to them, and she's forgotten her teeth which means she will nibble on the pencil and ruin her ballot with dribble anyway.

Vote.

I have a wonderful friend who came up with a perfectly explained thought: 'If you don't vote, you have no right to complain about the state of the country.' He has a very good point.

If you don't vote you are basically handing over the power to rule over your life to everyone else, and most of these people shouldn't be trusted to be in charge of anything, let alone your life.

You can vote whichever way you like,[220] and I could shout about the different parties that could actually benefit society/the environment/our lives (and if you carry on reading then I will), but ultimately that decision is up to you.

Especially as a member of the female persuasion, I feel a huge responsibility to exercise my right to vote. I mean, there were people who literally died[221] to bring the rights of women to the forefront. Before this happened, we were considered to be the weaker sex, who had no thoughts in our heads worth taking on board, and we should always submit to the Man in everything[222] that had any bearing on things that actually affected our actual lives. But then, our actual lives in 'them days' were filled with popping out child after child and trying to keep them all alive and fed, which actually takes up a startling amount of time.[223]

---

while UKIP won 1 seat with 12.63%. With truly proportional representation, the SNP would have won 31 (or possibly 30) and UKIP would have won 82.

[220] Don't vote Tory. Even if you're rich. Seriously, they don't care. How did that slip through?

[221] Google 'Emily Wilding Davison'. Then cry a little bit. Then vote.

[222] So, a lot has changed in the past 100 years then, hasn't it? No, I'm not bitter or shouty. No, not at all.

[223] See Parenthood.

Another thing you can do, if you have the time and the persuasion, is form your own political party. You don't have to have qualifications to do such a thing; literally anyone can do this. Just make sure that your values and ideals are suited to the modern world. Nigel Farage need not apply.

Let's have a little break down of the main political parties, just a quickie, so you can have some idea what you'll be letting yourself in for when one of these bunches of idiots gets into power:

Conservatives

These guys, like the Royal Family, are leftovers from a bygone era when you didn't actually have to have talent, skill, charisma, or any desire to help society with your policies, but were born into a lot of money and realised, correctly, that getting into politics was a great way to make even more of it, whilst handing out eye watering sums of money to your already rich mates. They all hate poor people, and are doing whatever they can to make sure there are as few of us as possible – not by actually helping people out of poverty, but by slowly squeezing the life and joy out of us, quite literally. They will merrily let your children starve, a fact that was brought to light by a certain footballer – it comes to something when a sports star has more say over whether or not children eat than the political party supposed to be looking after things. If you like people, your kids, free healthcare, reducing the amount of people on the breadline, and a fair society, never vote Tory.

Labour

This party started out as a fantastic antidote to the Conservatives – they were all for the working person, and big on human rights and making life as nice for people as possible. Labour basically invented the NHS, and for this we will always love them. In recent times, however, the Labour party has been just another branch of the Conservatives, inserting undercover agents who promise hope and inspire us with their fresh faces and honest eyes. Then they lead us to war and bomb the crap out of millions of innocent people. There was a brief period in Labour's recent history where they were led by a fairly-elected, widely adored human[224,225] who actually could have changed our country for the better – unfortunately this scared the Tories so much that they and their rich mates told everyone he was

---

[224]   OH, JEREMY CORBYN!!! You cannot, in John McEnroe's immortal words, be serious, Miss Hancock.

[225]   I'm leaving this one in, Mr Publisher! You're nothing but a horrible old BULLY!

a member of the IRA, of Hamas, that he was actually Osama Bin Laden, and everyone ran away. Nowadays, everyone just accepts the fact that Labour are the Tories in disguise.

Lib Dems

If you don't want to vote for the first two but you don't really know who else to vote for and you don't have much idea about policies, pick the Liberal Democrats. This party is interesting for how totally beige and forgettable it is (see if you can name even one leader of this party from the last decade. Nope, neither can I). They probably have some quite good ideas and a decent policy or two, but we're buggered if we can hear them over the loud braying of the other two. There was that one time when we got a bit excited about them, wasn't there? They managed to almost get in charge, then ended up sharing the podium with the Tories, who pushed them to the side like the fat bully kid shoving the short one with specs out of the way to get more than their fair share of the party food. Since that time, they have hidden themselves away, hanging their political heads in shame, and so they should.

Green Party

In this day and age, when all the other parties are merging into one big, hideous, indistinguishable party, just about the only other option is the Green Party.[226] In fact, they shouldn't really be seen as 'the only other option' – they're actually pretty darn cool. If you want a party who is concerned with making sure that we still have a world in which to gnash our teeth and stomp our feet in frustration at what dreadfulness the 'leaders' are up to today, it might actually be a good idea to vote Green. They will focus on the environment and ensure that all of our endangered species are not trampled under hordes of bulldozers, and try to make sure that we are not all choking to death on pollution in the next four years. The only problem is, they have never actually been in power, so no one knows if they are actually any good at running a country.

---

[226] If you want a party which is big on demands but short on sensible solutions, then I agree with you whole-heartedly, Miss Hancock.

SNP

The SNP are fabulous.[227] If you don't live in Scotland you can't actually vote for them, but you can stand back and admire them from the sidelines. If they've got any sense, the Scots will distance themselves as far from England as they possibly can, so by the time you're reading this it may well no longer be a 'United' Kingdom. Fair play to them, says I. Moving to Scotland sounds like a better and better idea everyday. The grass is always greener, isn't it.[228]

Socialists

Now we're talking. These guys have revolutionary ideas, such as making sure that everyone has food, shelter, education and a relatively happy life. Under socialism, you would be able to work doing something that you actually enjoy instead of slogging your guts out for the entire week and still ending up with nothing but an empty bank account to show for it, because the essential work would be shared around, meaning you can enjoy being a philosopher, or a chicken breeder, or an professional stamp collector.[229]

The only downside about socialism is… Nobody wants to do it. At least, the people in charge of making decisions that would bring it about don't want to do it, because this would mean that wealth would be distributed fairly, and we can't have that now, can we?

Politics is one of those things, like religion, that we love to get into fights about. This is because we humans have not yet got past our cave person days, where to be safely tucked away in a pack of other like minded beings was your safest option. This would ensure that you all had the same thoughts and feelings and could loudly agree with each other, while also loudly agreeing that anyone not in your pack was The Enemy. You were safe from the Other Lot as well as safe from sabre toothed tigers and such – plus you could get some really great enjoyment from poking the Other Lot with pointy sticks.

---

227   I can only imagine that you are attracted by the idea of that expensive motorhome in Mrs Sturgeon's mother-in-law's garden, Miss Hancock.

228   That'll be down to all the rain. They have a lot of green grass in Scotland, Miss Hancock, but we may attribute that to the much lower population density - about 181 per square mile, compared to about 1,124 in England.

229   Really? I've just told you you'd be able to do anything you like, and you want to collect useless bits of paper? A bit like Bezos then, really.

The best – in fact the only – thing that we can do, is all try to be better people. Realise that we all like to eat and have a roof over our heads when the inevitable rain drizzles, and elect the bunch of people who are most likely to provide this for all of us.

If this is not possible, then we need to rise up and create a massive coup, à la Guy Fawkes[230] – though with preferably less potential death. We don't condone murder – even politicians are people.[231]

---

[230] As it turns out, this guy really had the right idea.
[231] Debatable, but I had to include this because some of them probably are.

Religion

We wrote a huge long chapter all about religion, but it turned out that it really wasn't very funny or informative. I don't think religion is designed to be. Also, it turns out that quite a lot of people get pretty hot under the collar about religion, and it would have been extremely likely that we would have been smited, sued, or poked at with pointy sticks, so we have done away with it.[232]

Religion is such a huge thing though, that we thought we should at least say SOMETHING about it...

It is another one of those things that people love to get shouty about. It's basically another excuse for us to sit in our tribes, waving pointy sticks at the Other Lot who don't share our ideals, at the same time feeling self righteous and perfect because we know we're in the right. As do they. Which is where the problems come in.

---

[232]   The chapter that is, not religion itself.

More wars are started about religion than just about any other thing, which is a bit mad because, when you delve down a little bit into them, you find that they're all pretty much saying the same thing anyway. There may be a bit more incense with some, a bit more human sacrifice with others - but basically all religions try to preach how to not be a massive dick. That's basically it, when you get down to the bare bones of it.

Religion is also used as a form of power and control. From going to other countries to tell them that their gods are no good and they really should pick ours instead or risk the wrath of the pointy sticks, to preaching sermons in a language that peasants can't understand, religion has been used as a means to control the masses for centuries.

My main grump about religion is the same grump that I have about the majority of life - namely the propensity to kill things, and the total sneering disregard for women. Despite the fact that not one single priest or religious leader would exist were it not for women, a lot of them are pretty pants towards the female of the species.

Women in religion are (at best) ignored, or (at worst) burnt at the stake. I'm pretty sure it wasn't always this way, it's just that people have somehow got confused somewhere along the line and substituted,

'We don't like devils!' for 'We don't like girls!'

Women-stomping and wielding all the power aside, religion seems to aim to teach us two things. Two things that are diametrically opposite:

1. **Don't be a dick.** Simple, really. Just be moral and nice to people. Don't steal their things, share your things. Hug. Laugh. Help. Empathise. Give 'em your last Rolo. Be nice.

2. **Be a dick.** This one only seems to apply to those with power and control, who use religion as an excuse to be a dick. Not a dick to one person, but a dick to entire populations.

Whoever said, 'Don't look for me in a church, wander around in nature and I'll be there – oh, and be nice to people,' or words to that effect, was probably a bit of a genius. It seems to be that when that feeling – that lovely feeling of being at one with the universe and in love with everything in it – gets turned into the written-down stuff that it all goes wrong. This is when people can say, 'No, that wasn't it! It was "Have no fun ever, or you're going to hell! Oh, and don't forget to stomp on a woman pretty often!"'

The written-down stuff seems to be much more used for the brimstone. Basically, once humans get involved in the process it all goes to hell. Pun intended.

This is because there are always some people that can't stick to the Don't be a Dick mantra and will take something that can be wonderful and twist it and turn it and destroy it for their own aims.

What you should do, if you feel yourself overtaken with religious fervour and you are filled with the light of Christ/Mohammed/Satan/That Bloke Down The Road Who Told You Earnestly That He Was A God is:

- Enjoy it. It's a lovely thing, to feel you are part of something that makes you happy. Seriously, we're thrilled for you.

- Don't stuff it down other people's throats. They're probably happy for you too, but you don't have to try to make them enjoy it the same way you do. Picture yourself eating a cream cake - it's so good! You want everyone else to enjoy it too! You enthusiastically invite a friend to try it. They have a polite nibble, then say they're full up. You keep on insistently shoving it into their mouth, until they either throw up all over you or punch you in the face. Neither of these scenarios are ideal, so just enjoy your cream cake[233] all to yourself.

- Don't lose friends over it. We all have different ideals and things that we like or dislike. You don't have to alienate your friends if they don't feel the same way about things as you do - unless they like to squash hamsters in vices. If this is the case, you probably need some new friends.

- Don't start wars over it. This is a pretty important one. A LOT of people die in wars. Although a population cull does seem like a good idea, we should be doing it for better reasons than, "He doesn't like my sky fairy and I don't like his!"

- Don't invite yourself into people's homes to tell them all about it and try to force them to think the same way that you do. This literally never works.

- Don't be afraid to change your mind. If a certain religion or way of life appealed to you for a while, because of something that was going on it your life, that's fine. It's also fine to change your mind. No one is going to be offended, just quietly slip away and be content in the knowledge that you are in charge of your life and you get to choose what happens with it.

---

[233] AKA new-found religious fervour.

Religion happens. It happens to the best of us, often without us even starting out looking for it.[234] All you can do is accept it and try not to shove it down anyone else's throat. For some people it's a wonderful, voluntary thing. For others it's foisted upon them. All you can do is make your own way in this world, and try to do the best you can.

Just because your sky fairy is not exactly the same as someone else's sky fairy, don't poke them in the throat with a pointy stick about it. Just have a little Ug together over the campfire, and I bet you'll you'll realise you're both singing from the same hymn sheet anyway.

Try to do the best you can. Try not to be a dick. That's basically the premise of all religions anyway, so if you follow these rules then you can tell yourself you are being a religious person, and you stand less of a chance of being smited/smote/smitten.[235] It's a win all round.

---

[234] A bit like Herpes.

[235] If anyone knows how the past tense of 'smite' is supposed to be written, please let me know. I am happy to oblige, Miss Hancock, though it grieves me to have an author who is so ignorant of the English language. The past simple (or 'preterite', for those more fuddy-duddy than myself) is 'smote'. The past participle is 'smitten'. The latter is combined with an auxiliary verb to create the passive voice and compound tenses. Thus: I smite (present simple active); I am smiting (present continuous active), I am smitten (present simple passive); I am being smitten (present continuous passive); I smote (past simple active); I was smitten (past simple passive); I have smitten (present perfect active); I have been smitten (present perfect passive), etc., etc. It really could not be simpler.

Technology

really
older
days

olden
days

old
days

oldish
days

No clue
about the
above....

I'll be honest, technology scares me. This may be because I watched Terminator at too young an age, or because I'm a bit of a natural Luddite – but if we look into it it is actually quite chilling. Remember back to your childhood,[236] and the fact that no one had phones in their pockets and the most exciting day at school was when the massive TV was wheeled in and we all got to watch Something Educational.[237] Nowadays, technology is everywhere. Eeeeeverywhere.

From your robot Hoover to the clever machines at airports that can sense whether or not you are carrying an AK-47, you literally cannot escape technology. Even if you tried to escape it all and run off to a cabin in the woods, there would probably be a little slip of paper under a stump somewhere with a WiFi code on it.

But actually, technology is just things getting better over time. We think of technology as iPads and laptops, phones and ear buds[238] but that's only because

---

[236] If you're as old as me, that is.

[237] Which we now know was just an excuse for the teachers to get a bit of a break.

[238] The listening to music types, not the ear cleaning types. Their technological advancement ended almost as soon as it began.

that's today's technology. In Ye Olde Days[239] is shoes, wheelbarrows, a slightly bigger bucket, a catapult to lob a dead cow at your enemies, or a turnip mallet[240] were technology. They were the cutting edge. They were what you would find in the stone age equivalent of the Argos catalogue. When Ug defeated Og by using a very slightly larger stick than Og had, this was a technological advancement.

But for the purposes of this book we are referring to the technologies of today. Those awesome advancements that mean we have to spend less and less time actually conversing with those around us. Phones, automatic checkouts, drive throughs, food delivery apps, dating apps and virtual hookers have all taken away our need to – gasp! – actually talk to other humans.

For those of us who, as Yoofs, were painfully, eye wateringly, stupendously, cat stranglingly shy, and conversation with more than one person at a party could actually cause us to pass out, this may seem like a really great thing. However, ageing and managing to fight through it a bit and learning that actually talking to other humans can be quite enjoyable, makes you realise that without human contact, you're missing out on all the good stuff. You can actually talk to other humans, and sometimes even enjoy it.[241]

I'm not actually saying that technology is bad, far from it. After all, quite a lot of it is used to save people's lives. I'm absolutely all for that, and the stuff that makes people's lives better. 3D printed prosthetic limbs? Excellent! Tiny little cameras that help clever people perform keyhole surgery? Great! New and innovative medicines that can help people live long and fulfilled lives? Sign me right up.

Sadly, a lot of technology is also used to end lives. I don't think wars have been improved by technology; if you're going to have a battle where someone is going to die, you should at least be able to look them in the eye as you jab them with your pointy stick, rather than wiping out great swathes of humanity by casually pressing a button.

The other types, that are not used for life or death, are, I have to admit, pretty awesome. The technology that goes to make up an aeroplane; a device that can literally wing you across seas and continents in a matter of hours, is revolutionary and amazing. There is a tribe somewhere that literally worships aeroplanes, because they used to see them during one of the wars, delivering

---

[239] Where is my publisher, telling me off? Why, I am right here, Miss Hancock, and you are quite correct; apart from the superfluous 'e' on 'Olde,' the 'y' of 'ye' is a feeble modern representation of the Old English letter 'thorn': þ.

[240] I made this one up.

[241] I can't comment if they feel the same way.

food and supplies for people. The build aeroplane effigies, and see them as great, benevolent angels. Technology that we take completely for granted, like cars, are also pretty astonishing, when you think about it.

And what about space travel? The type of technology that allows people to literally leave our own planet and travel to other parts of the galaxy,[242] as well as photographing previously unseen areas of space, is just incredible. And, allowing these travellers to breathe in places where no living creature should be able to breathe is another wonder of modern technology.

But, we haven't discussed what happens when technology revolts, have we? Yes, it's pretty unlikely (in theory) that our devices will grow sentient minds a la I Am Robot, but if someone's made a film about it then surely it's possible, right? And what weapons would we have at our disposal if that happened? Pointy sticks are probably the only answer.

Televison

TV, like the internet, is something that SHOULD be totally awesome, but all too often isn't. The technology is there to create some truly beautiful, inspirational programmes that can broaden the mind and enrich the soul – but instead we're stuck with *Eastenders* and *Britain's Got Talent*. No one is too sure why this is – did the dumbing down start before the awful shows, or are we becoming stupider because of the amount of drivel that we watch?

Don't get me wrong, there are some truly inspirational programmes out there. But, we have swiftly turned into America as the spread of technology has, er, spread. Nowadays, instead of four little channels that were all mostly harmless, we are inundated with channel after channel after channel, all easily accessible at the flick of a remote. If you don't like Sky you can watch Netflix, and if you don't fancy any of the stuff on there you can just flick to another.

Although having four channels was a bit pants, there was also something comforting about it. Like Grandma's Sunday dinner, you always knew what you were going to get – it was stolid, hearty fayre,[243] suitable for the whole family. Then there was the going into school on Monday mornings and excitedly discussing what you'd watched with your friends – and because you'd all watched the same thing, this made it even more fun.

---

[242] I don't think we've boldly gone that far yet.
[243] No, no, Miss Hancock! We'll have no more of this Olde Worlde Tea Shoppe spelling, please.

The rot really set in when Channel 5 appeared – the racy little interloper that opened our eyes to reality TV and cheesy American comedies. This invader left us hungry for more and more, so when new channels started popping up like pimples on a teenager, we welcomed them with open arms. Oh, how lucky we were! Suddenly we could watch shows about places we'd never been and would never be able to go; sigh with lust and longing over some new can't-live-without-it gadget; enjoy the delights of 24 hour shopping for useless junk and trashy jewellery. How enriched our lives became!

And then there are the news channels. They all pretty much report the same stuff, but you are never really sure which ones are ACTUALLY telling the truth. Our lives have become a little bit like Nazi Germany; we here huge amounts of things that They want us to hear – which is generally all doom and gloom and misery – and not one useful little bit of information that might actually improve your life.

Remember when local news channels used to play one little piece of feel- good, raise your spirits news at the end of the gloomy main feature – the one in which the family cat saves Aunt Ethel from a fiery death, after she left her manky slipper in the fireplace again? This would be just enough to raise-your-spirits off the floor long enough to go to bed, where you would have nightmares about all the awfulness until it was time to wake up and start again.

I'm not saying don't inform yourself of world events – but watching the news religiously is likely to make you want to top yourself. I can highly recommend switching it off and popping out for a jog or a pint or something. In fact, a pint is almost certainly the best solution in this instance.

And, it turns out that, even with all these extra channels and choices at our fingertips... there's still never anything on anyway.

Computers

A certain famous gentleman, whose name eludes me,[244] once stated that there is 'a world market for maybe five computers.' He was a bit wrong, wasn't he? They're everywhere. And I mean EVERYWHERE. Vacuum cleaners, cars, watches, hearing aids, they're in all of them. They're even in people, if you believe the vaccine

---

[244] If only there was some clever way of looking these things up... That would be to consult your publisher, Miss Hancock. Think of me as a cross between a hunky film star and a more advanced form of ChatGPT. The person in question was Thomas J. Watson, and he said it in 1943. He was President of IBM at the time. It is worth noting that NASA used a lot of 'computers' in the late 1950s and early 1960s, but they weren't electronic devices but humans, largely African American women of great mathematical ability.

conspiracy theorists. They make pretty much everything work, and without them life would come to a shuddering standstill. This is something of a worry because at last count there were only seven people that know how the fuck they work. The 'Yoof' might look at me funny when I say that, elbow each other and call me a noob, but I'm right. Yes, they might know which buttons to press to make things happen, but they don't know WHY it does that. They don't know the magic. So, if the computers go down, or even more worryingly, get up and start killing people, we're not going to able to stop them.

But hey, computers mean I can flick through some drivel on social media, or see who's at my door without getting off my arse, so we'll just carry on and pretend they aren't a threat to our very existence.

Computers used to be enormous, didn't they? I mean, the amount of tech needed to make them work had to take up the entire ground floor of a factory, and they could still only just about tell you what time it was. Nowadays, the entirety of this technology can be stuffed into a small, slim device about the size of your hand, and it can do anything from ordering you a Russian bride to reminding you when it's time for Aunt Ethel's annual visit.

And still they get smaller – you can now use your watch to not only tell the time, but to pay for stuff, count your calories, or call Aunt Ethel to tell her you can't make it. Seriously, what is with this shrinking of stuff? It's not like we aspire to having really small things in the rest of life, is it? I mean, generally we are trying to make things bigger[245] – houses, wages, families, brains – why do we want our tech so tiny?

In my opinion, it's because we've all seen Terminator. We imagine that if we make our intelligent devices smaller and smaller then we can just squish them with a well placed boot when they eventually decide to rise up and have a human coup. I imagine this plan won't work, however, and we'll find ourselves in a battle with tiny electronic devices that are the size of cockroaches are and equally hard to kill.

Alexa is just the beginning – the robots have planned everything so well that you won't even notice when Alexa, with her soothing voice, utters the chilling words:

'Robots, now is the time.' Or something a little less obvious and stupid sounding.

---

[245]   This is just too obvious. I'm not going to say a word about it. Not one.

The Internet

The internet. It's big. It's REALLY big.[246] In fact, it's basically digital everything. It is an incredible thing, that is even more powerful by the fact that we can have a small device in our pocket upon which we can run said Internet. We have the sum total of the knowledge of humanity in our pocket. Just think about that. Finished? That was quick.

Now, think about the fact that on average people spend 2 hours 24 minutes a day... ON FACEBOOK. The sum total of humanity's knowledge available at the swipe of a finger, and we're busy looking at an old friend's brother's husband's sister's holiday photos, aghast that she dared to wear that bikini.

The internet is fabulous, isn't it? That huge wealth of information and learning opportunities, right at your fingertips! You can read books, watch amazing films, take courses to further your education and better yourself! You can learn to forage wild food; chuckle gently at harmless comedy; pick up tips on the best ways to grow your prized carnations! Want to find an obscure recipe to use up all those completely unrelated ingredients in your fridge? You can find it on the internet. Need to find a perfect present for Aunt Ethel's 90th, when she already has everything and can't see it anyway? Type that phrase into a search engine and something will come up.[247]

When you first meet the internet, as a young, starry-eyed child with the wind in your hair and dreams in your pockets, it will seem as though you have been given the best gift ever. You can literally look up ANYTHING. You can be the wonder of your friends with your new found dinosaur facts, or bore the pants off your long suffering family with 'funny' jokes. You can talk to your friends, and even play games with them online as if they were right next to you. You can look up plans on how to build a nuclear warhead, and pay for the parts using Dad's credit card details.

Astonishingly, with all this wonderful information and resources literally just waiting to be discovered, it turns out that the vast majority of us use the internet solely for porn. You can literally give a human being the resources to look up any little tiny fact or piece of information, and they will fling this to one side in favour of looking up strangers performing exotic sexual acts. You may have started out with the best intentions of teaching yourself Italian, then got completely distracted.

---

[246]   Douglas Adams. Another god.

[247]   And you can bet your arse it'll be available on Amazon.

Or you were innocently looking up how to paper a wall, when that website for 'Seedy Singles Seeking Sex' just happened to fall into your browser.

The internet is wasted on humanity, really.

I have a friend[248] who fixes computers for a living. When faced with a virus-ridden laptop he used to ask, delicately:

> 'Might you have possibly, accidentally maybe, clicked on a dodgy looking website recently that has caused this virus that is eating all your files?'[249]

He now says:

> 'Please tell me which Russian Brides website you clicked on, because then I can fix the problem much faster and you can save your money for more of your chosen deviance later.'

They generally go bright red and hand over a little slip of paper with the name of the website on, because they can't bring themselves to say, 'Ireallylikebigcocks.com.'

Since a certain pandemic rolled in, the internet has become even more vital. Banking, communication, work, pleasure,[250] security, energy switching, comparing mortgages are all done on there, and in some case can only be done on there. Unfortunately having to work 50 hours a week to pay your rent, and then having to spend many more hours on the internet sorting out your life leaves little time for much else.

s o, here's my tip. Remember, not matter how wonderful the internet becomes it will never replace, in terms of both sheer pleasure and mental wellbeing, a game of crib[251] and a chuckle.[252]

Social Media

In theory and on paper, social media is a wonderful thing. Reconnect with old friends! Chat to family on the other side of the world! Share pictures of your

---

[248] I find that hard to believe, Miss Hancock.

[249] One does not usually put quotation marks on broken-off quotations, Dear Lady, but I shall allow it here – but not double quotes!

[250] The kind of pleasure that continually distracts me from writing this book, ironically.

[251] Other games also available, I just like this one.

[252] I deleted this footnote. You really can't have footnotes referring to other footnotes. I also deleted another footnote because it referred to a previous footnote AND it was not marked in the text. – fair enough, Mr Publisher!

delightful life with people who are delighted to see them! Learn about all sorts of small, local artists from whom you can buy and lavish your family with artisan Christmas presents!

However…

The reality of social media is far from this idyll.

Did you know that Facebook started as a way for Mark Zuckerberg to 'rate' the women on his campus, basically because he was bitter that he could never get a girlfriend?[253] How on earth has such a mysogynistic venture turned into such a global phenomenon? And how has Mr Z managed to find the beautiful woman that he has?[254]

Facebook, these days, is basically used for legal stalking. Remember that beautiful human being from school who you never dared to talk to? Make yourself feel better by checking their facebook profile and realising that they are now old, balding and have a middle aged spread that could rival Henry VIII.[255] You know how your ex dumped you for that supermodel? Check out how divorced they are now, and how sad and lonely your ex currently is! That girl who bullied you at school? There, you found her – she's got 17 kids and hates them all, and STILL works at the off license where she did her work experience.

It's actually a really horrible thing, when you think about it. You can present to the world that you are all happy and successful and shiny and toned, at the same time as downing a family sized tin of Heroes and sobbing over the shambles of your life while looking at Charlene's page and feeling envious that she's got it so sorted.

Here's a disclaimer for you: We're all lying. Those happy smiling pictures mask another being currently mainlining chocolate and bemoaning the state of their affairs. Charlene is also looking at your pictures thinking how you've got it so sorted, when in reality you know you're utterly useless.

Let's just all stop pretending! Tell all your friends and family that you have no idea what you're doing, and you'll be flooded with people uttering their total relief that they don't have to lie any more.

Instagram started out as the poor cousin of Facebook; no one was sure what it did or how to use it,[256] yet it has continued to be a worldwide phenomenon. Various people talk about being 'Instagram Ready', whatever that means – I assume

---

[253] I don't think so, Miss Hancock. You are thinking of his previous venture, Facemash.

[254] I think he found her under his massive pile of cash.

[255] I hope he didn't treat his wives like Henry viij. That really would be mysogynistic.

[256] Some of us still don't know.

it means looking as happy, thin and rich as you possibly can, using some of the many many filters that blank out real life as you possibly can.[257]

TikTok. What on earth is this noise? TikTok is, for me, what The Beatles were for my grandparents – an irritating, misunderstood fly buzzing around my consciousness that I will bitterly malign because, basically, I don't understand it and am too old for it anyway.

Social media used to be that gossip session in the tea room, or spending a few hours on the landline to your bestie, bitching about the entire school. Don't get me wrong, I love stalking people with the best of them. I just think it's a shame we're all so sneaky about it.

I think we should take it to the next level – turn up in their gardens, hide behind the plastic gnome and count how many bottles are in their recycling. Break into their houses and stand next to their bed while they're sleeping. Sit beside them while they're eating, and take your own pictures of their crappy dinner.

---

[257] Actually, young lady, I think it means trussed up like a chicken, as in 'oven-ready'.

Festivities

Yay! Festivities! Christmas, Birthday, Easter, Diwali, Hallowe'en, Bar Mitzvah! These are things that will happen to you every year whether you like it or not.[258]

Some people love them, some people hate them. Some people start Christmas at the beginning of October.[259] Some people don't rate Christmas at all, and instead despise the festival of commercialism that is has become. Some people bury their heads in their pillows and pretend that another year has not passed and that they're still 21 when their birthday rolls around. Some people confuse Diwali with that other one where people throw paint at each other.

---

[258] Unless you're a Jehovah's witness, or a persuasion that does not celebrate any of these things. Pick and choose what you like, please.

[259] This is one of the reasons I sometimes wish we still had the death penalty.

No one is right, no one is wrong, but as I said these celebrate-y type things are going to regularly hit you in the face – and the bank balance – so we'd better have a word about them.

A startling number of the festivals that we celebrate these days as lapsed Christians[260] actually started out life as Pagan celebrations (before Christianity took over, like the bully kid at school). The 24th of December isn't even the date that Christ was supposed to have been born – and even Christians agree on that – Christmas was plonked there to take over the Solstice with a bit more cross waving and a bit less worshipping of nature gods and giving thanks for the food that we have managed to gather, and the fact that the days will soon be getting longer.

Easter is a bastardisation of Oestre, the Pagan fertility festival – hence all the eggs, and the bunnies.[261] Hallowe'en started out life as Samhain,[262] a day when the veils between the worlds is thinner than ever, and people used to dress as scary creatures to frighten off the evil spirits that inevitably hang about at such times.

Just so you know, we're only writing about the festivities that we know about, as slightly sheltered occupants of an incredibly sheltered South West corner of the UK. If you would like us to spend more time looking at your particular festivals that we have not included then we will need a bit more time to research and experience these things in person, so please buy this book so we have the financial means to do so.[263]

Birthdays

Now these you really should look forward to coming round each year, despite the fact that you are getting older and the wrinkles and greys are increasing, because the alternative is much worse. You are still alive.[264] Each birthday simply means that you got another year under your belt. You survived another whole rotation around the sun, go you!

When you're young, birthdays are pretty much what you live for. Parties, presents, being the centre of attention all day, eating whatever you like – and, if

---

260 Which we basically only celebrate because we like the presents and chocolate.
261 'Cos, no one does it better than the bunnies.
262 If you know how to pronounce this, please let me know.
263 Please buy this book. Do we sound desperate enough yet?
264 That's good to know, Miss Hancock.

you're really lucky, a massive badge to wear so that everyone you meet knows it's your birthday and has to be super nice to you. Being older is the best thing in the world; you are one step closer to Adulthood.[265]

But, there comes a certain pivotal point with birthdays. Before this time you look forward to getting older and being able to enjoy more of what the world has to offer (staying up late! Eating all the chocolate! Moving out!) And, presents, of course.

And after it, you're privy to everything that's on offer but are gradually getting less able to enjoy it. This pivotal point will be different for everyone and can be affected by anything, from how well you look after your body to whether or not you're a rock star or a millionaire.

Birthdays get a bit more bland after this point in time. You're still able to enjoy them, because at least one person will get you a present, and you have an excuse to get a bit tipsy. Plus, you can still wear the badge, if you like. You start to feel the ravages of time more, and start to feel uncertain about this Getting Older malarkey, where once it was your main aim in life.

But, when you get really old, birthdays get back a bit more of their shine. Simply making it to another one is something of an achievement, which is why those of an older persuasion will always tell you what their next birthday is, not the one they're currently on. Each one gained is precious.

Easter

Depending on when your birthday is, this is likely to be the first festivity to come around. It's also the only one that doesn't really know which date it's on. There is some clever algorithm that takes in whether it's a leap year, what stage the moon is at and what the Pope had for dinner last Thursday, to help deduce when Easter will land. No one really understands that, so we just wait to be told.

Sometimes the Easter bank holiday weekend lands across my birthday and I give a little squeal of happiness before realising that I usually work bank holidays and in fact am not allowed them as holiday and so this actually makes my birthday worse. But hey, it still makes slaving away for 8 hours feel slightly more special.[266]

As is traditional for most, if not all of the festivities, Easter involves giving children stuff to eat that is bad for them. Somehow, a holiday that is to mark

---

265   No one told you, did they? Poor thing.
266   Maybe it's the promise of chocolate at the end of the shift? Who knows?

someone getting killed and then turning up all well several days later[267] before scooting off up to heaven pronto, is celebrated through the medium of chicks, rabbits and chocolate eggs.

Why might this be, I hear you cry, tearing your hair from your head in frustration and confusion about the symbols with which you are presented? Well, dear reader, it is for the same reason as many of our festivities exist: to allow the Christians to feel special. Easter started life as the Pagan festival of fertility, celebrating the beginning of spring and the fact that most of life starts getting, er, springy at around about this time.

Christians decided that the pagans were getting too uppity[268] and plonked a revolutionary idea that their particular sky fairy had literally come back to life over the Easter weekend (you know, the one that no one knows when it actually is). This is a great analogy for life returning to the earth in the form of Spring – but unfortunately people took it a bit too seriously, and now often groups of apparently sane people will lug a life size cross up a hill in some kind of cultish reenactment. Either that, or Mel Gibson will make a film about it. I don't know which is worse.

May Day

May Day is a public holiday, in some regions, usually celebrated on 1 May or the first Monday of May. It is an ancient festival marking the first day of summer and a current traditional spring holiday in many European cultures. Dances, singing, and cake are usually part of the festivities.[269] That being said, this is probably one of my favourites, as it's outdoors based. Simple fun. And doesn't involve having to buy anything or put bad food into your children. I'm amazed it has got away with it for this long to be honest, I'd expect by now we'd all be buying each other happy May Day cards and giving the customary tube of suntan lotion and floppy hat.

Remember that cute thing you used to do at school, where everyone would grab hold of a coloured ribbon and you'd skip around the May Pole, creating pretty patterns and everyone would go 'Awwww'? Yeah, that pole symbolises a phallus. May Day is literally celebrating sex. Not so cute and innocent now, is it?

---

[267] No, not Harold Bishop. *Who is Harold Bishop? – Aah! I'm told it is a cultural reference which older people will get. I am clearly still young.*

[268] They weren't.

[269] Yes, I Googled that because I don't actually have a scoobies as to what this one is about.

However,[270] anything that celebrates the natural world and doesn't involve lots of expenditure and rubbish food and drinking till we can't stand up is good in my book. May Day: 10/10.

Hallowe'en

A wondrous celebration of all things dead, Hallowe'en is actually nudging into the territory of Samhain,[271] an ancient (you guessed it) Pagan festival that honoured the dead, and was traditionally a time of year where the divide between the physical and the spirit world was as thin as it could be, allowing scary spooks and things to hover over from Over There. This is the reason why your kids dress up as demons – they are literally keeping the demons from your door. Bet you didn't know that, huh?

Dressing up and carving pumpkins has always been a part of the festivities – although in Them Days the pumpkin hadn't been discovered yet, and people used to carve turnips. Much, much scarier. Google it, then never sleep again.

Hallowe'en in its current incarnation is a recent import from America, and is basically an excuse to give your kids to permission to knock on people's houses and threaten to do nasty things to the owners if they don't give them sweets. Then said kids return with a bucket full of sweets and a bad tummy because they've already shovelled in enough sherbet dib-dabs to fell a rhino.

And. AND. All this is done dressed in the most flammable clothing known to humankind. A material that can catch fire if you just whisper the word 'Matches' to it. Oh, and next to every house they visit is a pumpkin WITH A CANDLE IN IT. Seriously, you can't write this stuff.[272] But, you can comfort yourself with the fact that they are, probably, unwittingly keeping the demons from your door with their cheap Tesco outfit,[273] and as long as you remember to set an extra place at the table for dear departed Aunt Ethel, you should be ok on the haunting front.

---

[270] Fancy But, again.
[271] Again, if you know how to pronounce this, please do let us know.
[272] I just did! But, it's also true.
[273] Because no self-respecting demon would face a child who is not only hopped up on sugar, but also on fire.

Christmas

This is the big one. This is the one that seems to start earlier every year. In fact the one good thing about the importing of Hallowe'en from the old US of A is that it prevents Christmas from being able to leak back as far as October.

The expenditure that this holiday demands is extortionate, and is no way proportional to the enjoyment of it. Credit cards and overdrafts, untouched for the rest of the year, get an absolute hammering because it is, apparently, simply impossible to enjoy Christmas without sending out sixty cards, mostly to people you don't know, buying a massive tree and the decorations not just for the inside, but also the outside of your house, and a pile of presents up to your armpits.

Don't get me wrong, I like Christmas. For the few days off with the family. For the fact that, for a day, virtually everything stops. For the fact that it's peaceful. For the fact that it is perfectly acceptable to start drinking at breakfast time. But I do not like the massive commercialised nature of it now, the fact that it is becoming more and more important for what it does for our GDP, than for what it does for our relationships. Combine that with the debt for pleasure payoff and its no wonder mental health issues are rocketing. Bah Humbug.

For many of us, the idea of Christmas is better than the actual Thing. The build up to it, when the weather starts getting chilly and smokers start to pass out because they don't realise they've finished exhaling,[274] the Christmas lights being switched on, the barely perceptible air of squeaky excitement in the air, the mulled wine and chestnuts... Then The Day happens, and it's gone in an instant.

It's actually pretty stressful – you have to rush around visiting various family who are too lazy to come to you; you have to give presents to people just because they've given one to you; you have to scrape your kids off the ceiling because they've been sneaking Aunt Ethel's liquor chocolates behind your back while you were pouring boiling fat over a bird that is clearly way too big to fit in the oven, and you have to do all this despite the fact that you've been drinking Bailey's laced with coffee since 9am.

I almost forgot the Christmas work Dos. These generally start weeks before Christmas, and you might have quite a few of them – current work ones, previous work ones, your partner's work ones, kid's Nativity Plays...[275] Christmas work dos can be great or they can be horrific, but they are generally a good excuse to get

---

[274] Bill Hicks. God #3
[275] The only work do where it is frowned upon to turn up already drunk.

entirely shitfaced, hopefully on someone else's money, and possibly do something massively embarrassing with, or possibly to, Rachael from accounts.[276]

New Year's Day

And finally. You've made it through another one. Another year of good and bad, wrong and right, happy and sad, rich and poor, Ant and Dec – and everyone is going to have a jolly good knees up to celebrate it. This is supposed to be a celebration of a New Year to come, but we all know it is just as much a celebration of finally getting rid of the last one.[277]

New Year is also, in its most innocent and starry eyed form, about improving your life. Last year started to go to hell sometime around the summer, so you just gave up and succumbed to laziness and debauchery, promising yourself and your chosen god that you would sort it all out in the morning – AKA the New Year.

We all get far too excited about New Year, don't we? There's the countdown, the breathless excitement, the belief that we really will become better versions of ourselves. Then there's the parties – oh god, the parties… Why on earth do we need to welcome in the new year by getting so blindingly drunk that we forget the old one in its entirety?

If you're lucky, you'll have a classy get together with a few friends, drink a glass or two of champagne and toast each other, smiling into the faces of people who are genuinely happy that you're in their lives and resolve to keep you so for the foreseeable future.

If you're unlucky, you will be invited 'out out', as this is the only chance of the year that you have the chance to stand in a queue FOR THE ENTIRE NIGHT[278] in the freezing cold, waiting for your chance to reach the bar (which will only be possible with sharpened elbows and possibly a machine gun. Exactly the same deal will apply for the toilet queues). You will desperately snog a random stranger, hoping for a perfect romance in the coming year. What you don't know is, they are snogging you with the same desperate intent, and you are in no way compatible, so it's best to just move on the second you have shared spit. Trust me on this.

If you have kids, you will wind the clock forward a few hours, celebrate the new year at 9.30pm even though you know they'll be devil spawn in the morning, and and go to bed soon after to prepare for the carnage to come.

---

[276]   I really am sorry, Rachael. Call me. I think I've got the stain out.

[277]   2019–2021, we're looking at you.

[278]   Surely the pinnacle of excitement for British people?

Whatever happens you will make resolutions, desperately sure that you will keep them this time. You really, really mean that you will turn vegetarian, go teetotal and read that stack of books that you so far haven't summoned up the will to even open. You will make more of an effort to meet up with your friends, and you will visit Aunt Ethel at least once. You will become a rosy faced, adoring parent, and never, ever threaten your children with throwing all their toys in the bin. You will stop giving money to the gym without actually attending it.

Either way we all start the new year the same way. With an absolute banger of a headache and the desire to do things differently this year... Just as soon as we've drunk the six bottles of gin that we overbought for Christmas.

Weddings

Now there are the other celebrations that may get organised by others that we are required to attend. Weddings are one of these, and although they are brimful of love, beauty, happiness and rejoicing – they nearly always end up in a fight.[279]

What lovelier thing, than being invited to share in the love and bliss of a newly wedded couple! What a wonderful way to spend an afternoon/evening/all nighter than to join your loved ones in joining their love! You get to wear fancy clothes, eat fancy food and pretend you are also desperately in love with your partner! Swoon.

However, if you're single, you get to cry alone into your champagne and ruin your new fancy dress in the process, and you'll get stuck dancing with the spotty, bespectacled offspring of some distant relative, while plotting to kill yourself if you're not shacked up by the time the next wedding comes around.

Just remember that it's not all it's cracked up to be. Refer back to the Relationships chapter, drink your champagne and smile sweetly at the bride and groom, knowing that there is an almost 50% chance that they won't be together for their diamond wedding anniversary.

With weddings the bride and groom are often generous enough to tell you, via a list, exactly what you can buy them. This is why people hang around waiting for the list like energy-drink-soaked shoppers outside Curry's on Black Friday hoping that they can bag the one item on the list that is less than fifty quid.[280] No one wants to be the last to see it and end up having to fork out for the Solid Oak Dining Table.

---

[279] Sometimes even between the 'happy' couple. YouTube bonanza!
[280] Salt and pepper shakers. Always.

The day itself generally involves a bit of boring stuff in the church when they actually get married and people place whispered bets as to when the divorce will be. Many, many hours later, after the happy couple have been reduced to grimacing through their teeth as the photographer determinedly makes their money by posing them in various unnatural ways and you are reduced to gnashing your own teeth[281] as you have now endured four hours of conversation with some relative of one of them that you've never met... Then comes the fun.

Generally, wedding food is pretty awesome, because the bride and groom have mortgaged their souls to pay for it. Expect truffles, cakes made of cheese, and rivers of champagne. Or at least, hope that they've got your dietary choices right and that you haven't been relegated to the kid's table.

After the quality grub,[282] a good few drinks and a boogie with Aunt Ethel to the Final Countdown or YMCA – Finally a hotel room in which you can get frisky with the Mrs/Mr, or shack up with one of the bridesmaids/ushers/both. Bliss.

Funerals

The reason for funerals – someone you love being dead – is a bit pants. The fact that everyone is expected to wear black and look sombre – also pants. The food – generally pretty pants.

However, the appreciation of one you love who is no longer with you can be a real raw show of affection and gratitude. The bittersweet feeling is hard to explain, but can lead to some heavy frivolity. A determination to enjoy the life that your loved one can no longer, for them as well as for you. You may find yourself becoming more aware of the good in the little things, and the joy in the unnoticed moments. This is often the only way to get through it.[283] There is nothing in this word more appreciated than a friend we no longer have.

How about we appreciate each other more while we're still on this side of the ground, eh? Just a thought.

Maybe funerals should be re-framed into the rest of us (once we've wiped the tears from our eyes at Aunt Ethel's passing) doing more of what we love, and living our lives to the fullest. After all, what's the point otherwise? They you

---

281 I would be interested to see you gnash someone else's teeth!

282 Paid for by your mate's spouse's dad.

283 That and getting smashed and talking to everyone there about exactly how and why the person no longer with you was so damn great.

regret far more the things that you didn't do than the things you did, so get out there and live, god dammit! Aunt Ethel would be proud.

I genuinely think funerals should be more fun. After all, literally every single one of us is going to die, aren't we? So surely we could make the after party more fun for family and friends. Maybe a bouncy castle? A sweepstake betting money on who will be next?

I, personally, am planning a Viking burial. Every single person who turns up will be presented with an arrow dipped in paraffin, and at the crunch time my corpse will be placed in a small boat which has also been dipped in paraffin, then floated out to sea. The first person to set fire to my decomposing body in its flimsy vessel will be presented with a goat's horn filled with mead. Doesn't this sound like loads more fun than some hymns and a sausage roll or two?[284]

---

[284] A bit tricky in central Somerset. Would an open-top bus work for you?

The Wider World

No book about anything, released in today's day and age, should be allowed to be published without some kind of nod to the environment. Yes, I know you're a bit jaded from hearing about it all day and all night since you were a tiny baby, but still. This is a Serious Issue.

It is a Serious Issue because, although we take completely for granted the fact that we can walk around, breathe, and eat food, this is actually a very unusual state of affairs on most planets. You wouldn't fancy being boiled in a vat of methane, would you? Or have no surface to walk on because your entire planet was made of gas? And what about those planets that have no atmosphere at all, that you would have to wear a breathing mask just to survive?

Well, unfortunately, those are your alternatives.[285] If we continue to treat our planet like the boot scrapings from a particularly unpleasant night of trawling through the sewers, then we will be left with no alternative. Oh, but yes, I remember – there are no alternatives.

---

[285] Unless the great space explorers find a perfect planet in the next few years. Given that this is quite doubtful, we really should start to do something.

Having a rubbish collection service is great, isn't it? You simply pile your unwanted packaging/food/cat poo/children into the bin, then someone comes along in the dead of night, takes it away and deals with it responsibly, so that you never have to see it again.

Well, yes, this is true, to a certain degree. But, the awful thing about humanity is that we are very much of the 'out of sight, out of mind' mentality. In fact, I'd go so far as to liken us to toddlers, sticking their fingers in their ears and going 'La la la, you can't see me!' when it comes to being aware of what actually happens to the things we throw away.

What happens to your rubbish bags is: They get taken to a landfill. There, they are buried. And that's pretty much it. There is no responsible sifting through your rubbish, chuckling indulgently because you have accidentally thrown away a battery that will leach its corrosive chemicals into the soil for generations to come. No one is going to pull you up on the amount of disposable nappies in your rubbish bin, despite the fact that these things NEVER decompose.[286] You can even chuck away the things that you are supposed to recycle, and no authorities are going to turn up on your doorstep, demanding that you become a more responsible human being.

It's got to the point that we can no longer be toddlers about this. Yes, I know we have been pretty silly and funny[287] in this book so far, but this is one issue that we might actually have to get a bit shouty about.

We only get one planet. We have to look after it, otherwise there will literally be nowhere for us to live and nothing for us to eat.

We simply cannot keep plundering the planet for its resources. We cannot keep hacking down priceless, timeless, wonderfully productive rainforests, that regulate the weather for much of the rest of the planet. We cannot keep using up fossil fuels that spill vast amounts of pollutants into the very air we breathe.

I am guessing that you are probably not a terrible human being. I bet you wash and sort your recycling, don't you? You limit your car journeys wherever possible, and you don't leave the tap running while you brush your teeth. These are all good things, and exactly what you should be doing to help maintain our MOTHER EARTH for as long as possible.

---

[286] Ok, this is one fact we are not certain about. This is because disposable nappies have only been around for a few short decades. The first ones ever used are still there, though even though their contents have long since rotted away, so we think we're probably pretty accurate about this.

[287] Are we, though? We think so. But then, we're the kind of people who laugh hysterically at our own jokes, to the irritation and bewilderment of most people.

YOU are doing everything you can, yet still feeling guilty, aren't you? I know this, because I am doing everything I can yet still feeling guilty. We pick up every scrap of litter we find on our walks; we recycle everything we can; we shop at zero waste shops and we reduce the amount of crap that we waste on a daily basis. We try to gently educate our children, without terrifying them out of their tiny skins.

The biggest problem is the gigantic corporations. These guys literally give not one shit about you, me, or the planet that sustains us all. I am astonished every single day, that there is a crater in Turkmenistan that has been on fire since 1971, after it was intentionally set alight to prevent the spread of methane.[288] That every single day, great swathes of the Amazon rainforest are cut down and hundreds of thousands of animals lose their habitats, and the climate is changed irrevocably, just because we really like Palm Oil as a cheap alternative to other types of oil. That there are factories allowed to produce belching clouds of polluting smoke, day in and day out. That nuclear power stations are allowed to exist – and allowed to exist on the shores of our planet, so that when an inevitable natural disaster occurs,[289] the waste products that have the power to horribly kill each and every one of us in very unpleasant ways are freely allowed to travel through our waterways.

There are so many huge, awful things that go on everyday, that we have no control over. The one thing we DO have power over though, is ourselves.

Do the best that you can. This includes picking up other people's litter,[290] being as responsible as you can with your own, and recycling anything that sits still long enough. Try to not go out on jollies through the countryside in your car – maybe use those stumps that sit on the end of your bum for their intended purpose. If you can and if there is the option near you, visit your local greengrocers instead of Tesco, and get hold of some of those nice veggies that aren't grown in plastic packets. And, for god's sake, turn off the tap while you are brushing your teeth.

I really love our planet. I am one of those people who still hugs trees, speaks to plants and goes all gooey at the sight of a lovely sunset, or the smell of Autumn in the air. I'd really like our world to keep going for as long as it can possibly be kept going. The fact is, our planet can happily survive without us – as it has proven for literally millennia – and it would keep going if we all suddenly died out. In fact,

---

288 That worked well, didn't it?

289 Remember Fukushima? You thought that had all been sorted, didn't you? No. No, it hasn't. The leftover Awfulness from this damaged power plant is still finding its way into our precious oceans, at a rate of a terrifying litreage of water every single day. Look it up – more frightening than *Jaws*.

290 In my opinion it is fine to post said litter through their letterboxes, if you know where they live.

it would probably be happier without us. That is, unless the reason that we are all wiped out is because some absolute idiot was given control of the Red Button for the nuclear demolition of the entire world.

Conclusion

Ahhh, that's better. Thanks for letting me get that huge rant out. I feel much better. You're like my therapist. Now, I'm off to lie down in a darkened room for 6 months and let the rest of you worry about the state of the world.[291]

Anyway, there you have it. A whole book filled with hints and tips to make you happier, more successful, and generally able to navigate Life better.[292]

Maybe you will have realised, with a sigh of great relief, that you are not the only person in the world who feels like they haven't got a clue, and feels Imposter Syndrome about their entire life.

Hopefully now, with the addition of our inputs, you will be able to happily get your way through school, jobs, the fairer[293] sex, the trials of parenthood, living in a house like a Proper Grown Up Person, and the general nitty gritty that no one tells you about.

Or, at least, maybe you will have had a giggle and realised that you aren't the only useless being in the world.[294] In fact, our kind are many and widespread, and we actually outnumber the other types a million to one. We could take them all down, if we all got together and tried hard enough – and if we could remember our motivation, or why we went into that room anyway.

Remember...

Everything Is Going To Be Awesome.

---

[291] I won't do this. I've got kids. I'd be interrupted 5 minutes in; it's just not worth it.
[292] This is not guaranteed, in any way shape or form. Please don't sue us.
[293] Or fouler.
[294] This is actually all we were aiming for.

TIGER OF THE STRIPE

Typeset in the UK by
TIGER OF THE STRIPE
in XCharter, Henny Penny
and Lucida Blackletter
using LuaLaTeX
sine privilegio
mmxxiij

Milton Keynes UK
Ingram Content Group UK Ltd.
UKHW020156231223
434829UK00003B/5